STUDENT PARENTS

The Essential Guide

Need
— 2 —
Know

Camilla
Chafer

First published in Great Britain in 2011 by
Need2Know
Remus House
Coltsfoot Drive
Peterborough
PE2 9JX
Telephone 01733 898103
Fax 01733 313524
www.need2knowbooks.co.uk

Need2Know is an imprint of Bonacia Ltd.
www.forwardpoetry.co.uk
All Rights Reserved
© Camilla Chafer 2011
SB ISBN 978-1-86144-104-1
Cover photograph: Dreamstime

Contents

Introduction

When people become parents, their children not only bring a whole new perspective on life, but they can also inspire their parents to realise dreams and ambitions. It is the quest to realise these dreams that has seen parents becoming one of the fastest rising groups amongst students, with the numbers of studying parents rising every year.

Research conducted by the National Union of Students (NUS) indicated that one third of students in England and Wales have one or more dependents. In Scotland alone, the figure for students with a young dependent was 10% of the student population. There are also many more young parents returning to schools and colleges. Additionally, parents are inspired to take up degrees and postgraduate study while many international students bring their families with them. Regardless of the course they take, all these parents are united by their desire to learn and the pressures they face while attending classes, handing in coursework and meeting the demands of parenting.

Despite being one of the fastest rising student groups, many student parents feel that they are not supported and have difficulty in accessing information, such as finance and housing, that could help them. Despite this, NUS research found that student parents were amongst the most determined to succeed. Simply put, student parents have a lot of responsibilities and fierce ambition to improve their lives, and that of their families.

In this book there are case studies of parents who have taken a variety of courses. Their stories will help motivate other parents taking their first steps in, or returning to, education. It will dispel myths about typical students, assess why parents make good students, look at how teenage pregnancy does not rule out higher education and find out how postgraduate study can be undertaken. Furthermore, this book gives tips on dealing with student life while managing parenting responsibilities, along with advice for academic success.

This book isn't just to help, support and motivate student parents though. It also contains valuable advice for those involved with student parents; including teachers, tutors, student union support staff, career guidance counsellors, partners, friends and families. By offering an insight into the demands of combining studying with parenting, those around the student parent will better understand the issues that student parents face, and will be better able to support them as they strive for their goals.

None of the students who kindly offered their time and their inspirational stories during the research for this book, said studying and parenting was easy all the time. However, they all said the rewards were immense as they worked towards reaching their personal goals and improving their family's prospects. Their message is simple: Go for it!

Disclaimer

This book is intended as a starting point for all parents thinking about, or undertaking, a course of any level. Alongside your own research, your educational establishment and local authority will be able to provide up-to-date details of any additional funding as well as guidance on the right course for you.

Chapter One

Who are Student Parents?

There are some strong ideas of what a typical student is. A typical student image is of late teens in university; partying late, lying in bed, racing to lectures, propping up the bar in the student union and rationing out their student loans from one term to the next. Yet statistics show that not this is not the reality for many students (Smith and Wayman, 2009).

Breaking down student stereotypes

If student parents don't come under that band, then who are they? They are a hard-working group of people, from young parents still at school or college to university students from 18 to any age above. They are parents who are taking their first qualifications, and parents who are taking graduate level courses. Student parents can be part-time, full-time or long-distance learners. They can be paying for courses and living expenses from their own money or may be entitled to government-funded loans and grants. In some cases they may be receiving benefits.

The NUS found that the majority of student parents are more likely to be women, mature students and part-time learners. However, the NUS also found student parents to be a very diverse group with a wide range of backgrounds, qualifications and commitments.

Just from this section, we can see that there is an enormous variety of student parents. What they share is a desire to learn, a motivation to better their lives and that of their families. They also face similar obstacles such as access to affordable childcare, suitable housing, parenting issues that conflict with study, such as childhood illnesses and school holiday cover, and a lack of support due to the limited research undertaken on student parents. These are compounded by issues that are similar to the stereotypical student, such as placing themselves in debt to study.

Student parents tend to show a determination to succeed. Studying and raising children can be strenuous, tiring tasks in their own right. Combining them can raise issues but can also contribute to a desire and determination for success. The NUS report found, 'student parents feel they have more to lose if they fail'.

How many student parents are there?

Research conducted by the NUS indicates that one third of students in England and Wales have one or more dependents. In Scotland, the figure for students with a young dependent was 8,700, or 10% of the student population, making parents one of the biggest rising groups of students. Despite this there is little research data available about student parents and many feel there is a lack of support or understanding about their situation.

Currently, academic institutions are not required to collect or record information about who has dependents, so it is not easy to see what support student parents are able to access and what else they might need to enable successful study.

What issues do student parents face?

Under 18s: The school-age mum or dad

Young parents are one of the most bad-mouthed groups in the UK. Figures are regularly touted in the media about 'feckless' children bringing new children into the world. Few acknowledge the burden placed on young parents who are trying to bring up their children while still continuing at school. It's no easy task and young parents who have the determination to continue in the face of adversity should be better supported. It is this determination that will ensure they do not become the media scapegoats.

'Student parents are trying to make the most of the opportunities available; they are an inspiring and hard-working group of learners, highly motivated by their family responsibilities and passionate about learning.'

Meet the Parents
(Smith and Wayman, 2009).

In 2007, there were 44,805 births (a figure almost half that of 1971) recorded for women under the age of 20. In the same year there were 8,196 pregnancies for under 16s, with around three quarters of those for 15-year-old girls. In 2006, only 4% of total births were to mothers between 12 and 18 years old (source: ONS Birth Statistics).

Young parents may have yet to complete their GCSEs and so be without qualifications. They may have felt disinterested in school and have a lack of focus. Their children may have given them a renewed focus as they are determined that their child does not 'lose out'. In a report from the YWCA, a charity which works with young, disadvantaged women, found that 83% of respondents felt that 'pregnant teenagers and young mums should have the same access to education and training as other teenagers'.

The job market is increasingly competitive. It is important for young parents to remain in education, even if it can seem difficult to do so in the short term, so that they are able to take advantage of the same employment opportunities that are available to their peers who have not become parents.

University students

In Meet the Parents, the first UK-wide study into student parents at university, conducted by the NUS (2009), it was found that the majority of student parents were female. They were often mature students and studying at home and were focused on improving their own and their family's lives.

University student parents may have had their children prior to starting university or may have found themselves pregnant while at university. At the youngest in this demographic, an 18-year-old student may already have a baby or child.

Alternatively, the student may be classed as 'mature' (over 21) and may have young children or older teens. They may have returned to university following a period of employment, unemployment or full-time parenthood.

While it is understandable that it is harder to study with a baby or toddler who requires much attention, student parents with teen offspring may also still be facing similar issues of access to finance, looking after their children and general wellbeing.

'I'd had a very difficult time at secondary school and hadn't wanted to study anymore. Shortly after having my son I realised that I wanted to study, and better myself, for his sake and mine.'

Hayley, 20, Access to Social Sciences.

Falling into this demographic are also parents who have become pregnant and given birth while at university. For them, university life may change drastically from living in student halls and having a typical student life to one where childcare and family housing become new concerns. These students may return to university immediately or may wish to take some time out. Male and female student parents may have different experiences of having a baby at university. They may find that they can share childcare, a home and continue to successfully study together.

Returning-to-education parents

Many parents return to education when their children are small or have just started school themselves. This group of parents may have achieved few qualifications while at school and been inspired to study for qualifications to enable them to improve their employment prospects. They may also be keen to provide a good example for their own children.

This group of parents may be starting off with access courses at local colleges or centres where they can gain the basics in English, Maths and ICT. They may be taking GCSEs or A-levels or may be taking access courses as a route to a university place.

They may be combining employment and parenting with education and thus may be long-distance learners or taking evening classes.

Long-distance learners

Many student parents cannot attend a traditional campus for lessons. Instead, they might be drawn to long-distance courses where coursework is sent to them for study in their own time and assessed by mail or via the Internet.

Long-distance learners require a great deal of self-motivation as they may be without student support and cannot just 'drop in' to visit their tutor. They may be looking after children or working during the day, while spending evenings and weekends studying.

This group may be able to access financial aid if they are at a lower level of income, depending on the course and institution they attend.

'My children know I study so I can get a better paid job, so that we will be able to do nice things together at a later stage. It is a bit of a juggling act, but do not be put off, because it is manageable.'

Nicola, 29, BA (Hons) Psychology.

Graduate students

Many student parents have taken the conventional route. They have left school, gone on to university and may even have enjoyed a period of time in the workplace before having children.

However, this group of student parents may be looking at furthering work prospects, changing their career path or may be returning to study after a period out of work due to child commitments for example. They may also be looking to entertain themselves by pursuing a new interest. This group may well be familiar with the ins and outs of study and have previously enjoyed student life. However, now they may also have many other commitments such as a mortgage and career to maintain, in conjunction with their roles as student and parent.

These student parents may have left work to pursue study such as a masters, doctorate or MBA (Masters of Business and Administration) and may be investing a considerable sum of their own money in their education. Or, this group may have their financial commitments met by their employer, especially where the qualification will have a bearing on the job they perform. They may be full-time or part-time, on campus or long-distance learning.

As you can see, student parents are a very diverse group of individuals!

Can student parents be successful?

The authors of Meet the Parents, (NUS, 2009) found that student parents are highly motivated, inspiring, hard-working and passionate about their studies. Furthermore, they have a determination to succeed despite the many issues they face and obstacles in their way.

Student parents don't want to succeed just for themselves, they want to succeed to improve the lives and opportunities that their children have. Students with children are very aware of how much education can impact on their lives and how that will affect their family. With this pressure, and ambition, student parents are motivated to continue their studies, even when faced with adversity.

How can teachers support student parents?

- Remember that student parents may be simultaneously raising children, working and meeting study commitments.

- Be prepared to help student parents with accessing support, such as finance, appropriate housing, childcare and dealing with issues of isolation.

- Be prepared to be flexible on deadlines if a plausible reason is offered (e.g. childhood illnesses).

- Don't schedule exams and assessments when childcare is unavailable (such as after 6pm, when a lot of childcare has ended, or early lectures when childcare hasn't begun) or help arrange for an alternative if a clash occurs.

- Sympathy – it can be tough being a student parent, sometimes they just need a sympathetic ear.

- Encouragement – a few kind words go a long way when students are feeling pressurised and under strain.

- Provide tips or support for effective time management and organisational skills so students aren't tempted to leave coursework until the last minute.

- Do not judge. You don't know why they are student parents, just that they are, so try not to make presumptions that may not be true.

- Remember that support from those around the student parent is important so they can continue to study, achieve qualifications and go on to successful employment.

'Ideally, support should begin prior to the arrival of students (with a pre-arrival pack containing organised, easy to digest, useful information) and would continue not only throughout the course but also for an extended period after students have left university.'

Siobhan Gallagher, Student Parents Movement.

How can places of learning support student parents?

- Schools, colleges, universities and other educational institutes should not be dissuaded from attracting student parents. Indeed research shows that student parents are motivated, dedicated and deeply inspired by their children to continue with their education. However, support for students could be considerably improved.

- Schools should actively encourage young parents to return to education and not discourage young women for health and safety or any other spurious concerns.

- Colleges and universities could provide an information pack, or dedicated website space for young parents with details of financial help, childcare and other aid available, such as housing. Along with a general pre-arrival pack that universities often send to new students, they could include details specifically for student parents, such as child-friendly spaces on campus, baby change facilities and play facilities. They could also host 'meet 'n' greets' for student parents and their children, enabling them to meet other students in the same position early on.

- Most of all though, sometimes student parents just want a kind word, encouragement and a sympathetic ear for the times when they feel that they have taken on too much. They can do it, but it helps if someone else believes in them too.

Summing Up

- Student parents are one of the fastest rising groups in further and higher education in the UK.

- Parenting is not, and should not be viewed as, an obstacle to study.

- Education can not only improve your prospects in life, but also that of your family.

- Study is only for a short time, but the skills stay with you for life.

- Student parents have many commitments; including study, work, parenting and family commitments. They can be successfully combined with determination and the right support.

Chapter Two

School and College Parents

Despite what the often sensationalist media may claim, there isn't a huge amount of pregnancies amongst young teenagers. Figures issued by the government show that by 2008, teenage pregnancies had fallen to their lowest rate in 20 years (Department for Children, Schools and Families/Department for Education, 2010).

Despite that, there are plenty of claims that pregnancy and early parenthood ends education. It doesn't have to be like that. Though early parenthood isn't an ideal combination with study, it can be done and can be the key to young parents leading successful lives, with good qualifications and improved job prospects.

Currently the law states that all children under 16 should remain in school. However, the previous government planned that from 2015 all parents under 18 will be required to remain in compulsory education or training, at the time of going to press it was unknown whether this will be enforced.

The first part of this chapter will explore how early parenthood and school can be combined to ensure that young parents don't miss out. The second part is aimed at those supporting young parents, including parents and teachers.

Pregnancy at school

School can be very difficult for some teens. Throw a pregnancy into the mix and, for some, it can seem impossible. Fortunately, we're making great strides towards not excluding young parents, especially young mothers,

'The 20,000 girls and young women under 18 who become mothers each year include some of the most vulnerable and isolated in society. If they drop out of education or training it will impact not just on their own future prospects, but on the life chances of their child.'

Dr Jane Evans, research and policy officer, Barnardo's.

from education. Some schools may want to carry out a health and safety assessment to assess whether it is safe for the young mother to continue to attend school safely throughout her pregnancy. In some cases this, and other objections, may result in the young mother being asked to leave school. Many young mothers report spurious reasons for being excluded from school such as no longer being able to wear the uniform or the school deciding that it is not safe for an expectant mother to attend. It can be hard to challenge these rulings but your local authority does have a duty of care to provide an education for anyone under 16 and you, or your parents, should press for continued education pre and post birth.

The government does not view pregnancy as a valid reason to prevent a young woman from accessing education. The law states that children must remain in school until they are 16, so your local authority has a duty to provide an education for you.

An important consideration is timing of the birth. Some young mothers are lucky enough to give birth to their babies in school holidays, minimising the disruption to their school schedule and giving them enough time to take care of their child and recover, before returning to school and without having to devote large chunks of time to study. Other mothers I have spoken to have had their babies in the weeks, or days, before exams and still been able to return to school to take their exams – and pass. This is largely thanks to the young mother's own resilience, determination and capabilities, coupled with the support she can be provided by family, school and friends.

School or a mother and baby unit?

Some local authorities have mother and baby centres, or special educational centres where a young woman can continue her education while also caring for her baby. In Northern Ireland there are School Age Mothers Projects for young women under the age of 19. These educational centres enable young mothers to continue to study for and take their GCSEs. Contact your local authority to find out what provisions are in your area.

'For many young mothers and fathers parenting seems to provide the impetus to change direction, or build on existing resources, so as to take up education, training and employment. Teenage parenting may be more of an opportunity than a catastrophe.'

Teenage Parenthood: What's the Problem? (Duncan et al., 2010).

Young fathers

Obviously, as a father, you do not become pregnant or give birth. You should continue at school and work towards receiving qualifications that will enable you to progress towards a good future. Many young fathers share in the care duties of their child and this can help both parents keep up with their studies. It's a good idea for you to discuss caring responsibilities with tutors, head teacher and parents. The school might be prepared to offer some flexibility so that you can meet obligations. By continuing with education, you are setting a good example for your children to follow as they grow up. Similarly, a couple who study together can support and encourage each other.

Childcare when returning to school

It is unsurprising that there are few, if any, childcare facilities at secondary school. If your child is born whilst you are in secondary school, childcare will need to be arranged within your family network or through a private facility like a childminder or nursery, the latter can be expensive and there is little funding to help with the cost. There is more information about the type of childcare that could be available to you in chapter 5.

Pregnancy and parenting at sixth form or college

On reaching sixth form or college, people of this age will already have some GCSEs and may now be on the path for A-levels, NVQs or other vocational qualifications. Sixth forms attached to schools are not usually equipped with childcare facilities but some further education (FE) colleges, which run similar courses and sometimes degree programmes, will usually have on-site childcare. At this stage, there is often less class time which can help with parenting responsibilities and you may be able to study during your free periods.

'Many mothers express positive attitudes to motherhood, and describe how motherhood has made them feel stronger, more competent, more connected to family and society, and more responsible.'

Teenage Parenthood: What's the Problem? (Duncan et al., 2010).

What financial help is available?

One of the biggest obstacles for young parents to return to education is the cost of childcare. In England, the Care to Learn scheme is specifically for the under 20s and offers up to £160 per week of childcare help (rising to £175 in London).

When you are at college, between the ages of 16 to 18, you might be able to claim Education Maintenance Allowance (EMA) which is a small payment to help you finance the costs of college. However you must attend college every day to receive the money, something that is not always possible for young parents who may need a more flexible approach to attendance. Young parents under the age of 16 will not be able to claim income support, though child benefit is always awarded.

However, there are problems with financial aid. In a report by Barnardo's (Evans, 2010), they noted an inconsistency in other UK nations (Wales, Scotland and Northern Ireland) regarding financial help for childcare. They also noted that financial help should not be cut off at 18, which can be detrimental to young parents who have taken time out to care for their baby and plan to return to education later.

'I hadn't wanted to study any more ever again after secondary school but after having my son I realised that I wanted to study and better myself for his sake and mine. Next year I will be studying Open University courses.'

Hayley, 20, Access to Social Sciences.

How can you support the young parent in your life?

The parents of young parents may feel an overwhelming sense of being 'let down' when they find out that their child is about to become a parent. They may be tempted to take over the role of 'parent' to their grandchild but rather than this being helpful it could interfere with the bonding process that new parents need to go through with a new baby. Financial issues could also be a big worry. It is important for parents of young parents not to let emotions cloud their judgement and remember that the support the young parent receives is vital to their education as well as becoming a good parent themselves.

If you're the parent of a young parent, you can help support your child in their decision to continue with their education in a number of ways. Consider the following:

- Can you offer emotional support?

- Can you offer financial support?

- Can you provide free childcare or assist with paying for it?

- Can you babysit during revision and exams?

- Can you offer practical guidance in looking for the next educational steps such as applying for college or university? Or can you find out how to take the next step?

- Can you help find out more information about financial aid or childcare support?

How can you support a young parent as a teacher?

When a young parent has returned to school or college, it may be tempting for teachers to revert to the idea that nothing has happened to them and things will carry on as normal. However, a young parent returning to the classroom will be dealing with a host of new things. They may be feeling anxious about their presence in the school, especially if they feel they are being gossiped about and judged by their peers, or they may feel that they have 'let down' the school and be concerned about having been left behind. They may be suffering from sleepless nights and anxiety about being separated from their child. All of these things impact on the way young parents study and this may need to be taken into account.

If you're a teacher with a young parent in your classroom consider how can you help support your school's goals, and those of the young parent, to help them leave with a solid education and good qualifications.

- Can you offer emotional support so that the young parent is aware that they are welcomed in the classroom?

- Can you offer practical support, such as providing them with an outline of lessons or topics that will be covered so they can read in advance? By having some knowledge of the lesson plan, this will help the young parent not fall behind when they are faced with sleepless nights and their other baby care responsibilities. Hopefully, this will also ensure that coursework is turned in on time.

- Can you offer any flexibility in your timetable? The young parent may not be able to attend on occasions, but may be able to read, study and complete coursework at home.

Case study

Jo had her baby when she was 16, returned to complete college and went on to university. She graduated with a first class degree in economics.

'I became pregnant in my first year of sixth-form college. My daughter was born during the summer holidays and then I went back in the second year. All my lecturers at college were really good and they were all very supportive. In my second year they let me miss a lot of my lectures so I only had to go in three days a week.

Her dad was still at school when I was pregnant and he was 15 when I found out. He did go to college but he gave up his A-levels so that he could get a full-time job to support us. He's since gone back to university and done a degree as a mature student.

Once I'd got my A-levels, I did the first year of my degree at my local college before transferring to a local university. I couldn't have done it without the support of my mum and gran at the time, helping with childcare and that kind of thing.'

Summing Up

- Young parenthood is not the end. With courage, resilience and determination, you can achieve your goals in life.

- Early parenthood does not mean you are at a disadvantage, but it does mean you will have more on your plate than the average student.

- Explore your options for financial support and childcare whilst attending school or college.

- Consider whether you will be able to attend a mainstream school or a specialist mother and baby unit.

- Don't rule out evening or weekend study if that is when you can get childcare.

- Don't feel this is forever – study is only for a matter of months or years and it will make other opportunities available throughout your life.

- If study seems to be too much to take on now, have a think about when you will be able to take up your education again.

- If you're the parent of a young parent, consider how you can support them – do they need emotional support, childcare or extra study time? And can you help with any of those things?

Chapter Three

Pregnancy and Parenting at University

Pregnancy at university is not the catastrophe it once was and it is certainly possible to continue your studies. You may choose to postpone your studies or you may be fortunate enough to have your child during term breaks with support in place to help with childcare that enables a swift return. The first part of this chapter assumes that you have made the decision to keep your baby and are looking at the options to find out how you can manage a baby and keep up with your degree. The second part offers more general advice for students who are combining parenting and a university education.

Unplanned pregnancy at university

If you have sex, you run the risk of pregnancy. It's a simple fact and it's one that still catches many people out. With unplanned pregnancy, of course, it is not always possible to have the baby at the most convenient time, say, at the beginning of the long summer break. Finding out the baby's due date is mid-term can be problematic but with a good support system, you might find yourself returning to classes very quickly and bouncing back to full health. You might also wish to leave university for a year out so that your baby is a few months older when you restart your studies. If you would feel better being closer to your family while your baby is young, you might be able to transfer to a university closer to home. However, you might want to stay at your current university and that should be possible too.

Planned pregnancy

If you are planning to have a baby whilst at university, you will need to carefully consider how a pregnancy and baby will impact on your studies. You will need to consider how you will afford to have a baby and study. You will also need to consider the time you have your baby and whether you can realistically recover from the birth fast enough to continue your studies. You should also consider whether you are willing to give up, or drastically reduce, the social side of university in order to have a baby.

Questions to ask

There are a number of different options to consider when you are pregnant at university:

- When is my baby due to arrive?
- Will I need to take time out for the birth and while my baby is young?
- Will I need to move to more appropriate housing and how much will that cost?
- How much is childcare? Can I access any financial help for that?
- Is there a nursery on campus or nearby? How soon should I apply for a place?
- Will I be bringing up the baby alone or with a partner?
- Can my family help support me financially or emotionally?
- Is it safe for me to attend university when pregnant? (For example, if your course involves working with chemicals or heavy equipment.)
- Will there be any/enough flexibility in my schedule to account for childcare, study, class time and any extra-curricular activities?
- Will my partner help with childcare or finances?

Should you stay or should you take time out?

This largely depends on when your baby is due and your personal circumstances. If you give birth during the Christmas or Easter breaks or during the long summer holiday, and have good, reliable childcare in place, you may find that you are able to seamlessly continue your studies. It is essential to seriously consider how your child will be looked after so you can attend classes. It is very rare that lecturers will let you regularly bring your child in to class it may be disruptive for other students. If you are unable to find suitable affordable childcare you should discuss your options with your personal tutor to find out if you should consider taking time out before resuming your course.

Staying together

Many long-lasting, loving relationships begin at university. This could mean your family too. If both of you are studying, you may be able to co-ordinate your timetables so that you have an equal share of looking after the baby, class and study time. However, don't discount extra help with childcare, whether it is with a registered childcare provider or family members. It's good to revisit the days when you could nip into the café without a buggy, round up books and study, or even just spend some time together.

Going it alone

Some relationships do not stand the test of time, regardless of whether a baby is involved or not. Don't be afraid of going it alone if you feel able to look after your baby and study. You may feel scared of what might happen, but you will soon get used to the change of pace in life and will feel very proud of yourself for successfully combining the two.

If you were previously in a relationship with the father of your child, you might be eligible for maintenance payments if he is employed. However, it can be a long, drawn-out process to make claims.

There are extra grants and loans available to student parents and you should consider applying for all that you are eligible for. These can help you with living expenses as well as costs towards childcare. You may not have very much money for the early years of your baby's life but this will only be for a short time. By finishing your degree you will be improving your employment prospects.

You should also be prepared for your ex-partner not wanting to know their child. This can be hurtful but the important thing is that you are there for your child. On the other side, your ex might want access to your child. If you are amicable, you should discuss when access visits can take place. If there is friction, you may want to consult the Citizens Advice Bureau or ask your university welfare office about legal help in order to come to a resolution.

Parenting at university

Student parents at university cover a variety of ages, from teenagers to older parents. These parents might already have one or more children before starting their degree and come from a range of socio-economic backgrounds. The things that unite student parents are their desires to pursue their education, gain qualifications and raise expectations of their family's future. Later chapters explore how to successfully combine parenting and education along with finding funding, childcare and more.

A note about childcare

Childcare is always one of the most difficult areas for parents. It is expensive, in short supply for young children and many childcare facilities will only care for a child over a certain age. You may even have to apply for a nursery place while you are pregnant to ensure a place for your child. Of course, you may have a partner or family close by who would be willing to help look after your child so you can go to classes. Inter-family childcare often works very well as you know the carer well and there may be few, or no, expenses. However, be wary of well-meaning friends who offer to help, if they back out at the last minute you will have no childcare. You may also be in violation of Ofsted rulings if friends care for your child on a for-profit basis (that is, if you pay them and they care for your child on a regular basis but they are not registered child carers). Childcare options are explored in more detail in chapter 5.

Finding family accommodation

Your accommodation needs may change once you have had a baby. If you have been living in halls or in a student house, you may find anti-social hours, noise and lots of people coming and going is not suited to life with a new baby. Your current flatmates may also not want to share a house with a newborn.

You may be able to rent a house for you and your baby and may be eligible for housing benefit to assist with costs. In many university towns you will be able to find information about rentable houses that are often leased as shared student houses. The fact that you will be sharing a house with a baby and possibly your partner, should have no bearing on whether you are a suitable tenant. You will generally still have to follow rent deposit and guarantor procedures just like any other student. You will also be responsible for all your own utility bills.

Universities often have housing suitable for families but these tend to be in short supply and high demand, so it is crucial to get your name on a housing list as soon as you know you might need such accommodation. Your student union's welfare office or accommodation office should have more information about this.

If you still live in your parents' home, you should discuss whether this is still possible with a new baby. You might find it convenient to remain in your parents' home and commute to university, especially if your family is able to help with childcare.

Finding support from your university

Do ask for support from your personal tutor. They might be able to put you in touch with other young parents at university who can give you a clue what life with a baby is really like.

Also ask for information from your welfare or student services office. They will be able to tell you about additional grants, loans or help that you may be eligible for when the baby arrives. They may also be able to tell you if there is a campus nursery or if there is any family accommodation available.

Case study

Gemma had her baby aged 20 and sat her second year exams a month later. She is now a qualified teacher.

'I found out I was pregnant in my first year. I went off at the end of summer with not very many people knowing I was pregnant and coming back in the autumn term quite heavily pregnant. I had my daughter in early December and sat my first exam a month later. I was told I could defer my exams and take them at the re-sits in August but I didn't really want to leave it. I wanted to give myself the option that if I failed I could re-sit them, but I passed them all.

There were a lot of people who really didn't think I'd manage university, they thought I would defer or give up, which I had never even considered. In a way that spurred me on even more because I wanted to prove them wrong.

My tutors were really good. I burst into tears when I told one of my course leaders, but he didn't see what the problem was. He saw no reason why I couldn't continue and he went through some of the options with me, like doing the exams during the re-sits or postponing them. I never felt discriminated against.

I felt a few times I had to explain that my boyfriend, who had just graduated, was working and we had bought our house. It wasn't just given to us on a plate. I got my student loan but I didn't get any benefits. My mum looked after my daughter for free so I didn't have to put her into nursery.

I think a lot of people think that once they've had a baby that that's it, and that you can't do things, and that there's no way around it. You can do it, things don't have to end just because you've had a baby.'

Case study

Camilla had her baby aged 18 and took him to university with her a year later. She graduated with an MA in European Politics and is the author of this book.

'I was pregnant when I sat my A-levels and knew that as my baby was due that November, I wouldn't be able to go straight to university. I wrote to my university and asked if I could defer my place for a year and they agreed. When I was 19, and my baby was 10 months old, we moved to university. There wasn't any help to find accommodation but I did get a nursery place at the on-campus nursery. I applied for the place while I was pregnant as I knew it was well regarded.

I only met a couple of other student parents while I did my degrees. Most other students found it quite interesting that I was already a parent and were quite supportive, though I didn't really partake in student life. I was often given information for mature students but as I was under 21, I wasn't actually classed as a mature student. I missed just about every social event, except for my graduation which my son came to. At times it was hard to keep going. We had very little money and I couldn't do the things I would have liked to have done for my son, but I knew I was working towards a better future for us.

There wasn't very much information advertised for student parents like me. I received the same student loan as other students, but had to find out what other financial help was available. My university were very generous and helped subsidise the childcare costs which were my largest expense. I really enjoyed learning and loved taking my son on campus. Occasionally I had to ask for help, like when my son had chickenpox and I couldn't meet an essay deadline but my tutors understood and I was careful not to abuse asking for help.

I'm very proud that I was able to successfully bring up my son and graduate. I wouldn't have the career I have now without that education.'

'One interviewee suggested that the lack of data about young parents is due to them "falling between two groups", being neither "traditional" students nor "mature" students, and this was backed up by what we heard from young parents in our focus groups.'

Meet the Parents (Smith and Wayman, 2009).

Summing Up

- Try to stay at university – it's only for a short time and you'll improve your employment prospects and financial stability for your family, when you have your degree.

- Ask your welfare or student services office about any help you might be entitled to.

- Think through your accommodation. Will you need to move? Can your university help you?

Chapter Four

Money, Money, Money

One of the most difficult problems facing parents who want to continue their education is money. It isn't just the cost of courses that can be a hurdle to overcome for student parents, but there are also the additional costs of housing, childcare and family living expenses. On top of that student parents will also need to budget for the associated costs of studying, such as books and materials, computing and printing costs. Many student parents will be unable to work due to childcare constraints and class commitments, leaving them reliant on financial aid from the government and other educational bodies.

Some funding is also available for further education students under the age of 20 to help them with the costs of childcare and other education-related expenses, such as travel and books. However, funding is rarely available for international or postgraduate students.

Many university students will also need to take out and repay loans after they have finished their course. Student parents can apply for loans in the same way a typical student can. Extra funding is available to help top-up student loans for full-time students, including maintenance and childcare grants to help with the costs of childcare.

Parents who combine work with study may also be eligible for help though the tax credits scheme. Additionally, postgraduate students may be able to access grants, though it should be noted that competition is fierce for a small number of awards.

'It's vital that students find out about the financial assistance that they are entitled to, such as tax credits, the childcare allowance for parents and free childcare which is available to students studying on certain NHS courses.'

Alison Garnham, chief executive, Daycare Trust.

How much will the course cost?

The cost of your course will depend on the institution, whether you are full or part-time and your age. School-age parents will typically be able to return to free schooling. Most FE colleges and sixth forms also offer free courses for school-age children.

Some colleges may charge a fee for mature students who are returning to education and this will vary for the type of course and the time it takes to provide it.

University fees are increasing but it is possible to take out student loans from a government scheme to pay for the tuition fees. You will be liable to repay the costs after your course has finished and once you are earning over £15,000 per annum.

Some providers, such as the Open University, distance learning courses and postgraduate courses, will charge a fee to take up their course. It may be possible to spread the payments of these courses and you will need to check that that option is available. Financial aid is more limited for postgraduate courses, see chapter 10 for more detailed information.

What benefits are available?

There are some government benefits available to parents but there may be restrictions such as the hours you study or work, how many children you have, their ages and whether you need to pay for childcare. Applying for benefits can be daunting and time consuming but try not to be put off.

Child Benefit

All parents are currently entitled to a weekly Child Benefit payment regardless of their earnings. You will most likely have applied for this when your child was born. Find out the most up-to-date rates and how to apply at www.hmrc.gov.uk/childbenefit.

'I was surprised and disappointed by the lack of government support offered to those who wish to return to education. There is a lot of help, both financial and practical, available if you want to go back to work, but very little if you decide to go to university.'

Claire, 25, BA (Hons) Philosophy.

Tax Credits

Tax credits are available to people aged 16 and over, who have at least one dependent child, and are in paid work for 16 hours or more per week. How much you receive depends on your income and you may also be entitled to Childcare Tax Credits too.

Childcare Tax Credit

This tax benefit is open to families who work 16 hours or more a week. Single parents will need to work 16 hours per week, while both parents as part of a couple will need to work 16 hours.

The payment depends on how much you earn and you can apply via the tax credits helpline or online via www.hmrc.gov.uk.

Housing Benefit

Student parents may be eligible for Housing Benefit if they can prove they have a low income. The money awarded is designed to help pay your rent. You will need to apply to your local council. Most students don't pay council tax and you will need to find out how to get this payment waived during your studies. More advice is available online at www.direct.gov.uk.

Income Support

You might be able to claim income benefits as a student parent. Couples may also be able to apply if one of you is not a student. Any other financial aid, such as maintenance grants and loans will be taken into account before a decision is made. You may have to sign on and off for benefits, for example at the start and end of summer term, and applications can be slow to process.

School and college

Care to Learn

Parents (mothers and fathers) under 20 may be eligible for help from the Care to Learn scheme. The scheme can help with childcare costs of up to £160 per week (£175 in London) and travel costs that are incurred by taking your child from your home to the carer.

The subject or course is up to you, as is the length of the course (be it days or years) and you can be full or part-time. The scheme is only available for courses in schools, sixth forms, sixth form colleges and other colleges, Entry to Employment (e2e) programmes, apprenticeships and community courses.

The childcare provider must be registered with Ofsted but you will be able to pick your preferred style of childcare, where available, including childminder, pre-school playgroup, nurseries and out of school clubs.

To be eligible for the scheme, the other parent must be unable to provide childcare and not claiming the childcare element of Working Tax Credit. You must start the course before you are 20, live in England, and the scheme will fund childcare until you have completed the course. The scheme does not affect benefits you or your family are in receipt of, but you don't need to be on benefits to claim it either.

The Care to Learn scheme does not provide funding for students at university or higher education courses.

Find out how to apply online at www.direct.gov.uk.

> 'At every college we visited it was reported that the money allocated for childcare for adult learners ran out early on in the year, leaving many students with children with no funding at all.'
>
> *Meet the Parents* (Smith and Wayman, 2009).

Educational Maintenance Allowance

The EMA allowance of up to £30 per week is available for children aged 16-18 in low income families. The money is offered to help you afford to stay on at school and can be used towards the costs of books, travel and anything else you need to keep learning. It's paid directly to you so you should think carefully about how you will use it.

The award doesn't affect any benefits you or your family may be receiving. You can also claim Care to Learn at the same time.

University – undergraduates

There are a number of financial help options that may help you with extra money towards childcare and other costs student parents incur. These are roughly divided between financial aid on offer by the government and university funds.

Access to Learning Fund

Students on lower incomes who are facing financial difficulty can apply for these funds via their university or college. It is available for undergraduates and postgraduates, full or part-time students. Student parents are a priority group for these awards and you can apply via your university or college welfare office once you've started your course. You should be prepared to prove your income (such as how much student financial aid you receive and bank statements) plus details of your outgoings, such as rent. You should apply for all other aid options before considering this. Funds are discretionary and can be offered as a loan or as a grant.

Only students in England can apply. Students in Scotland, Wales and Northern Ireland should contact their university or college's welfare office to find out if similar help is available.

Childcare Grant

This grant may cover up to 85% of your childcare costs and covers term time as well as holidays. Up to £148.75 per week is offered for one child and £255 per week for two or more children. You will need to be studying full time and have children under 15 in approved childcare. However, you won't be able to claim if you or your family already receive the childcare element of the Working Tax Credit.

You can apply for this at the same time as applying for a student loan and applications can be completed online at www.direct.gov.uk.

Parents' Learning Allowance

You can apply for the Parents' Learning Allowance regardless of whether you get the Childcare Grant or not. You will need to be a full-time student with dependent children. How much you get is means-tested on your household income but you won't have to pay it back. If you are awarded the Allowance, you could receive anywhere from £50 to £1,508 and the money is intended for use towards any course related costs such as books and travel. The payment is annual and you can apply every year you are in education.

Student Loans

This is the financial aid package that all university students typically apply for. It provides a Tuition Fee Loan to cover tuition fees and a Maintenance Loan, paid each term, to help support your living costs whilst studying. The money is a loan and so will have to be repaid once you finish your course and are earning over £15,000. You will need to apply every year that you are studying and you can apply for loans, grants and bursaries at the same time. Apply via Student Finance England. Part-time students should apply for the Fee Grant and Course Grant.

Student parents may also qualify for the Maintenance Grant which does not need to be repaid, or the Special Support Grant which does not affect income-related benefits.

Mature students

In this case, mature student refers to parents over 19 years old.

Adult Learning Grant

This means-tested grant is available to students over 19 years old and can pay up to £30 a week towards your costs. To apply for it, call the Learner Support helpline on 0800 121 8989 or ask about it at your college's welfare office. You can also apply for it before your course starts, but it will only continue to be awarded if you attend college.

Free Childcare for Training and Learning for Work scheme

This scheme is aimed at two-parent families where one works and the other wants to learn and develop skills that could help you get a job. The household income should be less than £20,000 per year. The fund can provide up to £175 per child per week (£215 in London) for registered childcare costs. You can study short courses or take formal qualifications

Family Action grants

Low-income families and those on benefits can be eligible to apply for grants typically of £200-300. Only those taking courses at Educational Grants Advisory Services (EGAS) colleges can apply. You can find an application form via the Family Action website.

Horizons Your Education Grant

This Barclaycard-funded grant offers help to lone parents in education. The scheme is UK-wide and typically awards amounts of £500-1,500. You can find an application form via the Family Action website (see help list).

Self funding

If you have enough money, it is possible to self-fund your studies. You should make sure you realistically have enough money to complete your course, taking into account tuition fees and living expenses. Under 18s should not have to pay any fees and most undergraduates do not self-fund as there is financial help available. However, many postgraduates do self-fund due to the competition for funding at this level.

Managing money

To help you manage your money, you should consider how much your incomings and outgoings will realistically be. If you are the person responsible for the bills in your household, you should work out how much you need to pay out for.

	Estimated cost	Actual cost
Rent/mortgage		
Electricity		
Gas		
Water		
Council tax		
Food		
Childcare		
Travel		
Clothing and shoes		
Books, materials and photocopying		
Computing and printing costs		
Entertainment		
TOTAL COST		

Student debt

It is a sign of the times that many students will have to put themselves into debt in order to fund their tuition and living expenses whilst studying at university.

Credit and store cards

It can be tempting to take out credit card after credit card to help fund your living expenses at university. It is not free money and should not be treated as such. You will need to make the minimum payment every month, though it should be noted that it will take longer to pay off the debt if you only pay the minimum payment.

Store cards typically have very high APRs (annual percentage rate, i.e. the cost of the borrowing expressed as an annual rate) and are not considered a good way of borrowing money. They may seem like an easy way to pay for store goods in the short term, but if they aren't paid off immediately, the interest repayments can rise very quickly.

Overdrafts

Many banks operate overdraft facilities for students. It is important not to view available overdraft funds as free money. Overdrafts often come with interest penalties (so you will have to pay extra money to use the bank's money) and can be recalled. You will also be liable to repay any overdraft money. Many students get into a cycle of becoming overdrawn when their loan money runs out but when they deposit their next loan instalment, that money is swallowed up by the overdraft causing them to become overdrawn again.

Summing Up

- Consider your incomings and outgoings. Will you realistically have enough money to live on?

- Ask your college or university for advice about grants and loans. They may know about funds that aren't widely advertised to students.

- Do not be embarrassed about claiming benefits. They are there to help you and it is nobody else's business as to whether you receive them.

- Beware of debt – look carefully at APRs and don't be tempted by credit cards, store cards and overdrafts. The money will all have to be paid back and you may end up paying a lot more than you originally borrowed.

- Don't be afraid to ask about money. Remember, if you don't ask, you don't get.

Chapter Five

Childcare

Finding suitable and affordable childcare is one of the most important factors for student parents to consider when deiciding to take up, and continue with, education. For students with babies and young children, it may also be one of your largest expenses.

There are a variety of childcare options available. However, some have pre-conditions, such as opening times and style of care, that you will need to consider when deciding which form of childcare will suit your family the best. Fortunately, you can often combine different childcare arrangements, such as family members with part-time nursery care or a school place with after school childminder care. In this chapter, we'll explore the different childcare options that will help you continue your studies while also having your child looked after.

Booking childcare can be problematic for many students. Childcare places generally have to be applied for months in advance. However, you might not get your timetable until the day of term. This leaves many students with the dilemma of do they book full-time childcare even if they might not need it, or book part-time care and find it is incompatible with lessons?

Informal childcare

Family

Members of your family who are willing to offer care for your child can often be the most suitable form of childcare. They may be willing to do it for free which will benefit your bank balance, and may be more flexible in the times they can offer you. They may be willing to look after your child in your own home, or, in

'We have no childcare. Neither my husband nor I, despite asking, received our timetables until the first day of the course, by which time it was impossible to find four places in childcare or after school clubs. If there are days when no one is at home for them, we take turns at missing classes.'

Penny, 37, BA (Hons) Applied Graphics Technology with Multimedia.

some cases, the home you share, which will save you travel time too. However, you will need to consider whether your family member is reliable enough, whether they have the time and provision to offer you long-term care and what you will do if they can no longer care for your child with short notice.

The pros

- Family childcare may be free, or at a reduced cost.
- It may offer more flexibility.
- Your child could be looked after in your own home.

The cons

- If your family member is unwell, you may need to find back-up childcare at short notice.
- You may feel beholden to them, especially if they don't ask for money.
- They might look after your child in a way you don't like, and not be willing to follow your rules.

Friends

Many friends have informal childcare arrangements. However, due to Ofsted rules, you may find it difficult to have an unqualified child carer, who does not live in your home, caring for your child and receiving any kind of benefit, such as monetary, in return for childcare. Additionally, you should really consider the reliability and character of your friend – it's not impossible that they may enter into an agreement with you to care for your child and then back out at short notice leaving you without childcare.

New Ofsted rulings say that friends can now provide informal, reciprocal childcare for each other. However, they cannot charge a fee for looking after your child. Your friend might consider registering as a childminder, giving them a job and you a valued carer for your child.

'Childcare is a crucial issue for both recruiting and retaining student parents. The decision to begin or return to studying is one that no student takes lightly – least of all a student with children.'

Alison Garnham, chief executive, Daycare Trust.

The pros

- Childcare by friends means someone you know, and your child knows well, will be caring for your child.

- They can possibly provide flexible care which could benefit you as your schedule changes.

- They may be more cost-effective than other childcare providers, or even free.

The cons

- Informal agreements are easy to break and can result in lost friendships as well as no childcare at short notice.

- You may run into potential problems with Ofsted and you will need to check the rules for childcare amongst friends carefully.

- Your friend might prefer for you to bring your child to their house which could add on travel time for you.

Formal childcare

Nursery care

Nurseries are a popular form of childcare for babies and children up to the age of five. Generally, children will be grouped together by age and will be looked after by staff with childcare qualifications. Children are encouraged to participate in activities together. From the age of three, your child will qualify for some free childcare through a government scheme. However, nurseries can be expensive, are often booked up months in advance and you may find that their opening times are limited. You might be able to find a nursery on your college or university campus, which might be financially subsidised for students, at a private facility or attached to a primary school. You may have to take milk and nappies for babies, on top of the nursery fees.

The pros

- Nursery care provides dedicated space for children with qualified, registered staff members.
- Even if one carer is unwell, the centre will still be open with other carers.
- There may be nursery care on campus so you won't be far from your child.

The cons

- Nurseries can be expensive and you might have to pay for your child's place even if you don't need it during holidays, such as Easter and summer.
- You will be limited to their opening times.
- You may be liable for fees even if you no longer need as much time as you originally booked.

Childminder

Childminders are registered childcarers who look after a small number of children of varying ages in their own home. They may look after babies as well as young children. Additionally, they might provide before or after school care for older children. Childminders are registered with Ofsted and will generally offer a varied programme of activities to keep your child entertained, plus their homes will usually have a child-friendly space and garden.

The pros

- A childminder may be cheaper than other forms of childcare.
- Childminders can be more flexible than other childcare options.
- Childminders look after a small number of children so your child may get more one-on-one attention.

'My childcare was paid for through an initiative for young parents called 'Care to Learn' which meant that I didn't have to worry about how to afford the childcare. I chose a childminder as it suited my son better. She has been wonderful; introduced him to new places and given him the patience he needs.'

Hayley, 20, Access to Social Sciences.

The cons

- There is only one carer who may be looking after multiple children, including after school collections.

- If the childminder is unwell, you will need to find alternative childcare at short notice.

- You will need to check when a childminder plans to be 'shut', i.e. for summer holidays so that you can plan ahead.

Nannies

Nannies are one of the more expensive forms of childcare. However, if you have more than one young child, you may find a nanny is cheaper and more convenient than nursery places. Nannies come in lots of different varieties.

Some nannies work full-time and others part-time, while some are available for a share arrangement where they look after your child and someone else's and the families split the cost. Some live with you, some live in their own home. Most will be prepared to care for your child in your own home. This also saves you travel time in dropping off your child before classes and saves having to collect them afterwards. Nannies are available through agencies, word of mouth or are privately advertised. You should always take up references. You will need to check if you are responsible for their tax, national insurance, sick leave and holiday pay.

The pros

- A nanny will generally care for your child in your home.

- Their focus will be solely on your child, great if you want one-to-one care.

- They may be able to offer flexible care, arriving earlier or staying later by arrangement.

The cons

- Nannies can be an expensive form of childcare.

- You may be uncomfortable having a stranger look after your child in the early days.

- You will need to be aware of employment rules and regulations and be a responsible employer.

Pre-school and school nurseries

When your child is aged three to four, they may qualify for a place at a pre-school or a pre-school nursery attached to a school. School nurseries are great for adapting your child to a school environment and familiarising them for the school that they will hopefully join the following year. They often do light teaching such as learning basic reading, writing and numbers.

The pros

- Pre-schools and school nurseries work well if you have older children already at the school so drop-offs are all in one location.

- Your child will be familiarised with the school they will eventually progress to.

- For school nurseries, you will only have to pay for term-time care, making the cost cheaper than other nurseries open all year round. Some of the hours will be paid for by a government grant which the nursery will apply for on your behalf.

The cons

- School nurseries generally follow traditional school hours of 9am to 3.30pm which can be awkward for early starts and late finishes.

- You generally won't have the option of childcare during school holidays.

- The nursery will not admit children who are unwell (regular childhood illnesses such as a fever or chickenpox) so you will need to make alternative arrangements in those cases.

Schools

All children are required to take up a school place in the academic year that they turn five, however almost all have a catchment area of addresses from which children are admitted so you won't always get your first choice. State school places are free, though you will need to pay for lunches (or provide a cold packed lunch) and small fees for other activities that the school has arranged that are in addition to the general curriculum, such as excursions and visits from various groups.

The pros

- School places are free.
- Your child will be in a dedicated education environment.
- Your child will generally be able to go to a local school, providing they are within the catchment and there are places available.

The cons

- You may need to make additional arrangements for the times your school is not open, such as before and after school and during the holidays.
- You will need to factor in travel time between school and your college.

School clubs

Many schools now offer breakfast clubs or after school clubs to provide wrap-around care for parents who can't drop off and collect during normal school times. These typically open for the hour preceding school and for two hours after school, though times may vary according to your school. The costs are often quite cheap and payable per hour. You may also have to pay a small fee (usually a few pounds) to register your child.

The pros

- School clubs are often run within the school so there's no extra travel.

- The cost is usually quite reasonable.
- Your child will be familiar with the environment and may already have school friends at the club.

The cons

- This type of care may not be available during school holidays.
- You will need to ensure you can return by closing time.

Holiday schemes

If you have nursery or school-age children you might find that your holiday times don't always fall in line with your children's. Many colleges and universities host holiday play schemes, often provided through the campus nursery, for the children of staff and students. They take a variety of ages of children and there will generally be a limited number of places so you should apply early. Some schools also offer a holiday scheme for their pupils, and those from other schools. There might be a charge for holiday schemes.

Funding childcare

Childcare may be one of your single largest expenses whilst you are studying. Many students find the cost of childcare one of the most difficult factors to consider when choosing whether to take up a course. Fortunately there are different types of funding available which you may be able to apply for, including:

- Employer voucher schemes.
- Childcare tax credits.
- Hardship funds.
- University welfare funds and subsidised childcare places.
- State-funded nursery care of 15 hours a week for the over threes.
- Privately paid.

How to find registered childcare

Word of mouth is one of the best ways to find a suitable childcarer, nursery or school. There are also a variety of organisations where you can find information about formal childcare including your local authority, Childcare Link and the Independent Schools Council Commission. Contact details for these organisations can be found in the help list.

Summing Up

- There are many different sorts of childcare available. You might be able to combine childcare to form the most appropriate combination of childcare for you.

- Try to finalise your class and study commitments as soon as possible so you will know how much childcare you will need.

- You might have to book more childcare than you think you will need to cover any unexpected class times. However, you might still be liable for any costs for time you no longer need.

- Ask your childcare provider if they know about any financial help available.

- Don't be put off by filling out forms. They are essential to getting funding and you might be able to get help filling them out from your student union.

Chapter Six

Student Life

A student parent may have a very different view on student life, and may have very different expectations, than the typical student. Not only will you occasionally find yourself explaining why you have a child, but you will also face extra barriers when making friends. Stress and guilt are often felt by student parents due to the demands on time, energy and finances. Here, we'll look at some atypical aspects of student life.

Children and study

Children and study do mix quite well. From babyhood, children have an innate love of learning and toddlers are like sponges, readily soaking up new information and skills. Many pre-schoolers will already be familiar with a small amount of schooling, such as practising pencil control or reading. School-age children will understand that in the same way they are doing homework, so are you. Many students cite their own studies as helping their children aspire to more in their own lives. The point is this: children will see study and learning as a natural part of their lives and so it is not an alien concept that you are studying too.

Explaining your situation to curious peers

Despite the large numbers of student parents, the idea is still an alien concept to many and you may find yourself attracting attention. They may be wondering just how you do it, how you find the time and how you are able to be organised enough to combine your two roles!

'I try to make sure my children know their support is valued and acknowledged. I always bring them to the end of year exhibitions so they can see what I have done and feel a part of what's happening.'

Penny, 37, BA (Hons) Applied Graphics Technology with Multimedia.

Conversely, you may also be the focus of some negativity from those who have not heard the phrase 'if you don't have anything nice to say, don't say anything'. They may be wondering why you have taken up studying when you are a young parent and what the point is when you're an old parent.

It's up to you how much you want to explain yourself, and whether you feel it is even necessary. You certainly don't have to tell anyone anything about your family circumstances, or your finances, if you don't want to.

Making friends and having a social life

Continuing your education not only opens up employment prospects but it can do wonders for your social life too. Indeed, many students thrive on the hubbub of campus and take as much pleasure in the recreational aspects of being a student as they do through studying. However, as a student parent you might find it difficult to develop a social life on campus while meeting all your other obligations. You may not have the chance to live in halls or a shared house and you might not have the opportunity to go for coffee after class if you're racing back to collect your child. Having a social life, an education and a child is a triangle that has no easy resolution. It is, however, important to try to make friends whilst studying. Not only does it make class time more pleasant when you have someone you are looking forward to seeing, but it's also handy for swapping notes, study sessions, not to mention pure and simple friendship.

Try to think of it this way, getting an education is not a popularity contest. You don't need to make hundreds of friends, do the Saturday pub crawl and have the cringeworthy photos haunt you forever after or even have fellow students jump up and down to have you sit with them. This is not high school.

Making a few good friends – or even one – or keeping up existing friends may be more satisfying. They may be the people you can turn to for a good moan, swapping notes or networking. They will understand if you can't make it out because you don't have a babysitter. Friendships like these are more valuable than making many acquaintances.

'As an undergraduate, most of the socialising revolved around the pub and I was only able to go along occasionally. To overcome this, I joined the Mature Students Association, which was an absolute lifesaver!'

Claire, 25, BA (Hons) Philosophy.

Need2Know

Many parents struggle with the different facets of their lives. When parenting and studying, there can often seem like little time or money is left over for enjoying yourself and having a social life. However, a social life doesn't always mean clubbing until dawn every weekend.

On campus

- It can be as simple as having a coffee before class with classmates.

- Going to the movies once a month – many theatres have student deals which makes going to the movies cheaper during the day.

- Lunch in the caféteria, or sharing a packed lunch outside.

- Meet 'n' greet – many universities are now putting on free sessions (often with tea and snacks) where you can take your child and meet other student parents. These are a great way to get to know people who might be sharing similar experiences.

No babysitter?

If you don't have family that are close by or willing to help out, babysitting is expensive. For many parents it can be a case of either having the money for a babysitter or having the money to go out.

Try hosting an evening in your home. Put the kids to bed, get in some drinks and nibbles (or ask guests to bring something to share) and have a nice time with some friends. It won't cost much and your friends may appreciate not having to spend a lot on a night out too.

Family fun days – meet up with other parents at a local soft play centre, park or your garden for a chat whilst the children play together.

Play dates at home – this is as much for you as it is for your children. Have friends over for a natter while your children play together.

Making friends online

Socialising online is a great way to ask questions, chat to others and ask for help – all without leaving the home. Many parents have turned to online forums to socialise, using sites such as Netmums, TheSchoolRun or BritishMummyBloggers. These forums allow you to discuss anything from parenting dilemmas to dedicated forums for students. You can even ask for book recommendations, local advice or offer opinions to others. You might even want to start a blog to write about your life as a student parent. It could be cathartic to write about your ups and downs as well as help you connect with other like-minded people.

Your college or university might have student specific sites for you to discuss course information or download class information.

University events

Many student parents feel very left out when it comes to big student events, such as the graduation ball, gigs and campus club nights. It's always worth trying to go along to an event and you might feel sad if you simply can't afford it and babysitting isn't available. Perhaps you and other student parents could host your own party?

Some universities are starting to offer sessions for students with families. Here they can bring their children along and mingle with other students. It's worth trying to make one of these sessions if your university holds them so that you can see that you are not alone. You might even meet some like-minded people.

Dealing with stress

When you have a lot of different areas of your life all vying for attention, it can become stressful. Work, study, children, social life and family obligations can all contribute towards a feeling of floundering at all, succeeding at none. Many students often feel like giving up when faced with so many demands on their time. However, it is important to bear in mind that study only lasts a few short years, while qualifications last a lifetime.

'The question we are asked most often by academic and union staff is "how do we get them to come to us?". Our answer is to give it as much publicity as you can and be patient.'

Siobhan Gallagher, Student Parents Movement.

Tactics for dealing with stress

- Put aside your work and take a break – have a cup of tea, go for a walk, watch some TV or read a book. Whatever it is, do something that relaxes you.

- Make sure you look after yourself – good sleep, nourishing food and some exercise all contribute towards a feeling of wellbeing.

- Plan ahead – good time management and organisation will ensure coursework doesn't pile up and help you feel less stressed.

- Make a list – what is making you stressed? How will you prioritise the list and how can you address the issues?

- Talk it out – does everyone around you seem calm and collected or are they bundles of stress too? You might be surprised once you start asking.

Coping with feelings of guilt

When you are studying, whether it is during the day, evening or weekend, you might feel like you should be spending time with your children. Conversely, when you are playing with your children, you might feel like you are neglecting your studies.

Many students feel that they are financially worse off by taking up studies to help them pursue a better life. Some might feel that they are depriving their children of new things such as toys or experiences such as day trips or holidays that they might otherwise be able to afford.

Due to the expense of education, some parents even feel guilty for taking a coffee break when they could be studying as they feel they aren't getting the maximum value out of their childcare fees.

These feelings are very typical of many parents and it's important to keep things in perspective. Both children and studying are important and both need attention, without being to the detriment of each other. Similarly, everyone needs some down time and giving yourself some time off to 'chill out' could be just the pep up that you need to keep ploughing on.

Summing Up

- Show your children what your work is. From babies to teens, you can talk to them about what you are doing and show how enthusiastic you are about studying.

- Don't try to pack too much in at once and organise your time well so work doesn't mount up.

- Accept that sometimes there will be timetable clashes and don't be afraid to ask for help to get around them.

- Don't be afraid to 'kick back' and enjoy some downtime. Remember the phrase 'all work and no play, makes Jack a dull boy'? Go and play and have fun.

- Make the first approach to other students. They might be feeling just as nervous as you, despite their calm demeanour.

- People may be curious about your dual roles as parent and student, especially if they have never come across a student parent before. It's up to you how much, or how little, you choose to tell them about your situation.

Chapter Seven

Combining Parenting and Education

Parenting and getting an education can be two full-time roles. Co-ordinating the two roles you have can throw up a unique set of problems. Unlike most students, you may have to deal with teething babies, sleepless toddlers and all manner of childhood illnesses. At the same time, there will be classes, essays and exams. However, with good time management and excellent organisational skills, the two roles can be combined successfully.

Making time for study

Study is best undertaken when you have time for free, calm, uninterrupted thought, note-taking and reading. Reading this, most parents have probably broken out in laughter. 'When do we have such time?', they might ask and they are right, it is difficult but it can be done.

Top study tips

- Study when you are feeling awake and alert.

- Choose a quiet time when you are not likely to be interrupted.

- Study elsewhere – if you are at home, you will be tempted by housework and anything else that looks like it needs your attention.

- Rewards – line up something nice up for yourself after a study session. Watch a film, read a book, get a magazine, have a bar of chocolate.

'Plan your time and stick to it. But don't just plan for study, plan time for family activities, or time for yourself to have something to look forward to. The quality of the time you spend is more important than how much.'

Penny, 37, BA (Hons) Applied Graphics Technology with Multimedia.

- Set up your study zone – have a drink, snack, notepad, pens and anything else you'll need so you aren't looking for things when you are supposed to be studying.

- Value your time – studying is an essential part of learning. It reinforces what you've learnt and the study time will benefit you in the future.

- If you can't find the time for quiet, independent study, encourage your children to study with you. Can they colour or read (in their head rather than aloud!) while you make notes?

Managing your timetable

Many parents find timetabling issues one of the most difficult parts of studying. Your set class times are generally inflexible; they are set prior to the start of term and continue for the period of study. Parents, however, find that their children are very flexible in terms of health. Similarly, many childcare providers are not interested in whether you have a class that falls out of the time when they are offering childcare.

Another problem for university students is that it is almost impossible to gauge when your next semester's class time might be. This becomes problematic when childcare must be booked weeks or months in advance to secure it due to high demand.

So, how can you overcome timetable and childcare clashes?

- It might be useful to book full-time childcare until you know what your hours will be. However, you may be liable for fees if you no longer need the hours you have booked, so you may wish to use time not in the classroom to study or enjoy student life.

- Only take classes that fit within your timetable. If a fantastic class starts too early or closes too late you may have to pass and find another optional class.

- Check before signing up to a class to find out if it is coursework or exam based. If it is entirely coursework, you won't have to worry about awkward exam times.

'Make yourself a study calendar and stick to it, even get ahead if you can, but definitely stick to your plan as far as possible. If you fall behind due to child illness or other reasons, catch up as quickly as possible. If you fall too far behind it can seem overwhelming.'

Nicola, 29, BA (Hons) Psychology.

■ Discuss concerns with your personal tutor. They may be able to help you find a more appropriately timed class or liaise between departments to find more appropriate times.

Dealing with deadlines

Young children generally do not understand deadlines. They also have a knack of becoming ill right before you have to hand in an essay which can make it hard to attend classes and find the time to write up coursework assignments. The easiest way to combat this is to do everything in advance. Start preparation for essays and other coursework assessments as soon as you are able to, including finding any material you will need. Early preparation should help you make sure that your essays and other coursework are finished in a timely way and ensures that you don't have to rush. Print your work at least the day before it is due in as printing problems are almost never accepted as an excuse for late coursework. This will also give you chance to proofread the hard copy.

Deadline extensions

However, your study schedule and other commitments might make it difficult to start early. In this case, you should not be afraid to ask for help from your tutor or course leader. Deadline extensions can often be given with plausible excuses and you should politely approach your tutor detailing why you are asking for an extension, along with any evidence to support your request, such as a medical note for a sick child. It is important not to abuse the extension system as repeat requests might be met with scepticism and turned down.

If you do not submit coursework as required on the designated date you may lose marks or not pass the course. You should always ask for a receipt for submitted work in case you need to prove it was handed in.

Coping with exams

The lead up to exams can be stressful and you will probably be asking yourself, 'have I studied enough?' and 'do I know enough about the topic?' Organise your study notes by class and date so that you can find them. Include any photocopies, handouts or extra materials in your notes folder so that they can be found easily. Most students have different systems for revising. Some might choose to revise as they go along, reading up after every class and making extra notes then reading through again at the end. Some might 'cram' where they intensively revise in the days leading up to the exam. Others might join a study group to compare and contrast notes with other students and to have the opportunity to test each other. You will find 'past papers' available through your student union or perhaps through the library or university online network. These contain exam questions from past exams and will give you an idea of how questions are phrased and will give you chance to plan how you will answer them.

On the day of the exam

Make sure you have a good breakfast so you don't have a sugar crash during the exam and prepare any materials you will need, such as pens, pencils, a drink and mints to chew quietly during the exam.

Approach the exam with the attitude 'I can do this!'. Read questions carefully, mull them over in your head and go for it. Immerse yourself in the subject and think through your answers. Think of a written exam like it's a piece of coursework with a beginning, middle and end where you introduce it, make your argument and conclude.

When the exam is over, relax and give yourself a little reward for a job well done.

What happens if you don't pass?

Relax. Not everyone passes every exam and the world does go on. You will generally have an opportunity to retake an exam in the summer term. If you don't pass a compulsory module on the first go, or during the retake season, you will probably have to retake the following year.

Consider what went wrong. Did you have an attack of exam nerves? Did you not answer all the questions, or not answer them fully? Did you not revise enough? What will you do to make sure that doesn't happen again?

What happens if I don't have any childcare during the exam time, or another clash?

Exam timetables tend to be made available with a few weeks' notice. However, all universities will be aware that there will, at times, be clashes (and not just due to childcare) and arrangements can be made to sit exams at other times.

It is up to you to make your department aware of any clashes. You should approach your tutor as soon as you know there will be a timing problem to see what alternatives they can offer. They will generally suggest you start the exam at an alternative time on the same day. It will take place in another room where several other students with clashes will also be taking other exams. You will be expected to not talk about exam questions with other students in your class until after they have taken the exam and you might find that you are not allowed to leave the 'clash' room until the rest of your class have entered their exam room.

Asking for help

Many people are reticent about asking for help. They might be concerned that they appear silly, weak or incompetent. However, asking for help means less time is spent floundering or worrying about something when there might be a simple solution that gets you back on track.

There are many people who you can ask for help. You could try a personal tutor, a course tutor or another staff member. Or you might try a family friend or online forum. If they don't know the answers, they might know someone who does or might be able to advise you how to research the problem. There are, of course, plenty of people who are unhelpful. Don't be put off by these people, just try to find someone else to help.

Helping children understand your studies

While babies and toddlers won't have any concept of what studying is, young school children will be able to understand in a limited way. Try to explain things in their terms. Just as they are learning how to read, write, do maths or use a computer, you are learning a new topic too. When they have to practise with their school books, you have to practise with yours. They will grow up feeling that learning and education is a natural state of business, something that is very positive.

Children can generally tell if you are feeling stressed, whether that is because you are tired, because you are studying for exams or are just under the weather. Sometimes the more focused you are on your studies, the more your child will 'act up' to get your attention. It will help if they know there is an end date when you will be more relaxed. For older children you can show them on a calendar when exams are and when holidays begin. For younger children, you can explain in simpler terms that 'in ten sleeps I'll have finished my essay and we can spend more time in the park' or 'I'll have finished classes when the weather is warmer this summer'.

Summing Up

■ Prepare for essays and coursework early in case of any unforeseen events, such as your child falling ill.

■ Ask for help when you need it. It is up to you to approach your tutor in plenty of time about deadline extensions or exam clashes.

■ Create a revision schedule to help you revise topics in the run-up to exams.

■ Be positive. A good attitude will benefit your mindset. Keep telling yourself you can do it.

■ If you don't pass your exams the first time round, remember the adage 'if at first you don't succeed, try, try again'.

■ Try to meet other students so that you are not isolated. It's nice to be on friendly terms with people you see regularly.

■ Don't forget that your child will want your attention too, set aside some quality time just for them. You might find it relaxes you to take some time out from studying.

Chapter Eight

Coping Skills

Many student parents find their experience of education to be isolating. While wanting to participate in wider student life, parents have childcare issues as well as general parenting dilemmas which often prevent them from doing so. This can cause problems for making friends, especially when moving to a new area, which can make parents feel very alone, and can add to existing stress. Many student parents contemplate leaving their courses at some point, questioning themselves if it is really worth it. However, there are ways to cope, it's certainly worth it and it's always important to keep the end goal in mind. Study is for a short period of time, qualifications are for life.

What to do when it all seems too much

Studying and parenting can seem like an overwhelming combination. On the one hand you have a little person, or people, who need clean clothes, good food, ferrying to childcare and play dates, baths and stories at bedtime – and that's just the basics. On the other hand, you have class time, reading lists, studying, essays and exams.

It is hardly surprising that sometimes you might feel like you are floundering or only just covering the basics. What is important is that you remember nothing is forever. Your children will not be so dependent forever and you will not be studying forever.

When it all seems too much, it is important to take a step back. That's not to say 'put your feet up and do nothing' – every parent knows that simply isn't practical. However, what you can do is take a little time out to recharge your batteries.

Five steps to tackle study stress

- Make a list – list everything that is outstanding. Don't tackle anything on the list just yet, but do be realistic about what needs to be done, what work is outstanding and when it is due. Prioritise in order of importance or in order of when work is due.

- Take some time out – now you know exactly what needs doing, put that list on your desk, or in your bag, and ignore it for the next hour. Don't think about it and don't plan how you will go about tackling each item. Take that hour to have a bath, bake a cake, go for a walk, watch some TV or have a coffee and stare at the wall. The aim is to clear your mind so that when you next look at the list you will feel more relaxed and more able to focus on things without feeling stressed. Taking time out is not the same as procrastinating.

- Don't procrastinate – social networking applications, email, housework, they can all seem a lot more interesting when you need to start a piece of coursework or swot up for your next seminar. However, putting off work may mean leaving it until the last moment when you might be tempted to rush it.

- Be organised – good organisation saves lots of time. Make sure notes are all in the same binder or in a folder on your computer so you can easily find it later. Have all your textbooks in the same place and ensure that any photocopies are kept with the relevant lecture and seminar notes. When you want to refer to them later, such as for exam study, you will have everything to hand.

- Get started – you can worry endlessly about your studies, or you can get started. Start reading, make notes or brainstorm an essay plan. Often getting started is the hardest part of studying and dealing with coursework and all too often students spend more time worrying about how to get started than putting pen to paper. Making a start gets you over the first hurdle.

Tips on staying the course

Continuing your education is a great investment. That investment isn't just in terms of money, but in terms of time, energy and determination. An education can help you improve your work prospects and, in turn, the prospects of your family, it can also contribute to self-fulfilment which, in turn, contributes to the happiness of your family. That's why it's important to stay the course, even when you wonder what madness possessed you to apply and when you feel that you just can't do it anymore.

- Remember why you started the course – what were your objectives? Did you want to learn something new, learn more about a subject you are passionate about or change your life in some way? Your desires are the reason you started the course and remembering them once in a while should help you recall why you are there.

- Have fun – education isn't about putting your nose to the books at the expense of all other things. Instead, you should take part, as much as you can, in the social side of life, whether that's joining a club or going to a café with other students. Having friends and a social life will help you feel part of something.

- The end goal – people generally study to improve themselves and often have an end goal in sight. Your goal might be to get a great job, it might be so that you can earn money or it might be so you can have a better family life. Keeping an eye on the goal will help you stay focused on your course.

Staying healthy

Looking after your body is as important as looking after your mental health. However, the last thing on many students' minds is balanced, healthy meals and a decent night's sleep. Yet, quite often, this is just what a student needs, especially when dealing with the demands of looking after children too.

Food

One of the benefits of being a student parent is the awareness that giving your child a diet of microwave meals and junk food is not conducive to a healthy body. Instead, many parents feel that they often eat better and healthier than they would as a single student as a by-product of making good food for their child. There are many studies that argue that healthy eating gives more energy, an increased sense of wellbeing, and a better defended immune system. Good nutrition is also good for the brain and helps you perform better mentally. There are many student-specific cookbooks but you will also find lots of recipe ideas online.

To keep your body in tip-top condition

- Try to eat a healthy balanced diet with fresh fruit and vegetables.

- Drink water to keep hydrated.

- Plan meals ahead so you can budget and shop without resorting to fast food.

- Don't skip meals, especially breakfast as it's an important start to the day.

Sleep

It's all too easy for a student without responsibilities to club all night, sleep a couple of hours and roll in for a lecture. You too might be experiencing sleep problems but if you have young, sleepless children, it's probably not your fault. Having your sleep interrupted frequently can feel worse than a self-inflicted lack of sleep. It can seem hard to decide what to do for the best. Do you go to sleep earlier and get woken more often? Or go to bed later so you are awake for late night wakefulness? It might take some time for your young children to develop a good sleep routine, which, in turn, aids yours but you will all get there eventually.

Seven to eight hours a night is the rough amount of sleep most people need and it's important to get enough to function well, be mentally alert and physically ready.

How to get enough zzzs

- Make night-times boring. Keep lights off, voices low and don't give in to the idea of the 'TV babysitter'. Make night-times so boring that your children won't want to wake up.

- Have a 'disco nap'. If you live close enough to campus, go for an afternoon snooze in-between lectures to catch up on some missed sleep. You might feel guilty because you are paying for childcare, but your good health will contribute to better studying.

- Have some wind down time. Don't study until your eyelids are drooping. Instead, put the books away, relax, have a warm drink and then drift off to sleep peacefully.

- Create a relaxing sleep environment with comfy duvet and pillows, snuggly pyjamas, blackout blinds and no distractions. And the same goes for your children.

- Have a routine. Put your children to bed at the same time every night with a story so they look forward to bedtime. Similarly, give yourself a bedtime so you aren't tempted to stay up when you know you will be tired the next day.

Exercise

Student parents may feel fairly stretched between the demands of parenting, studying and working, all of which leave little time for exercise. In addition, many university sporting clubs and activities are held on evenings and weekends when childcare isn't available.

However, there is exercise that you can do for free. Yes, walking. It might not sound particularly exciting but walking can help you keep fit. You could walk to and from your home to campus if it's less than a few miles (or just one way), 'park and stride' by leaving your car, if you have one, a short distance from the campus and walking the rest of the way. Pushing a pushchair is also good for a toning workout. Try searching the Internet for a pushchair workout that suits you. Don't forget that regular exercise will help your child get in to good habits from an early age too.

Learning to value yourself and your achievements

Many parents place value on everything but themselves. They are self-depreciating ('oh, it's only a short course'; 'it's just a degree in so-and-so topic'), ready to write-off any achievements as unimportant. Stop it! Your education is important. The process you will go through to get to the end, and the energy you will put into it, is important.

Valuing the day-to-day achievements you make, whether it is making a 9am lecture, handing in a great essay or completing your final exams, helps with the feeling that you are getting somewhere. Knowing that your children are being brought up well and that you are working towards a future that will benefit them is no small thing.

Keeping in touch with family

For some student parents, going away to university might be the first time they have left home. That they have their children, and possibly partners, with them is a boon but you might have homesickness for family and friends left behind, not to mention the familiarity of old haunts.

Technology has made it easier than ever to stay in touch with family and friends who may be far away. Although you might not be able to visit every week, a phone call home can be enough to lift your spirits and there are many calling plans available, including calling cards for abroad, that make calls cheaper.

Skype is a downloadable program that can be installed on your computer. It's free to download and so long as you have a webcam, speaker and mic (or a headset) you will be able to make video calls over the Internet. Other call charges might be payable. You can also use it for instant messaging. Your children will value seeing family that you can't see regularly and it's a great way to have a face-to-face chat even with hundreds of miles between you.

Keeping it all in perspective

When you first start your course, the end can seem very far away. Between taking your first class and receiving your qualification, there's an awful lot in-between – classes, exams, essays, reading and studying for weeks, months or years. However, whatever course you take, it will not continue for infinity. There is an end date.

If three years for a degree seems a long time, try looking at it in reverse. What were you doing three years ago? Does it seem like three years since what you were doing then and now? Actually, it probably seems like not much time has passed at all.

Think of the enormous sense of achievement you'll feel when you get your qualification. That moment of success will make all that studying seem worthwhile.

Summing Up

- Don't get to the stage where you feel overwhelmed.

- Be aware of your workload, when work is due in and how much time you will need to complete coursework.

- Have some down time but try to avoid procrastinating. When time is precious, it's important not to waste a lot of it on things that don't matter.

- Value the achievements you've made, no matter how small.

- Use Skype to keep in touch with family for face-to-face chats while miles away.

Need2Know

Chapter Nine

Your Choices of Education

Getting, or furthering, your education as a parent doesn't mean years of endless study or having to move far from home. Instead there are many options open, from short-term courses for fun, gaining recognised qualifications at a local college, to degree and postgraduate level at university. Many can be taken part-time or long distance so that they co-exist with your day-to-day life. Some parents even find that they get the academic bug once they have taken their first course and surprise themselves by going on to university and postgraduate study.

School

Parents under the age of 16 are required to finish school by law. Generally secondary schools are open between 9am and 3.30pm, or thereabouts, with a packed schedule of classes. Some schools might offer some flexibility to young parents. However, many will expect young parents to keep to the same timetable as other school pupils.

Further education

You may have missed out on GCSEs, A-levels, BTECs and NVQs the first time around. There are also other courses for skills such as English, numeracy and ICT skills, which can give you new skills or help develop existing ones.

You may even be inspired to take up a course whilst your child is doing their own exams. Or you may be taking the first steps towards university. Many local colleges are flexible with their courses and times, so it may be possible to study part-time in the evenings or weekends, or take a full-time course during the day when your children are in childcare or school.

For the under 18s, the courses are generally free and you might be able to seamlessly progress from school to college. Parents under the age of 20 are also eligible for Care to Learn funding which provides money to help pay towards childcare while they are on their course.

There may be a fee payable for adults for some courses at college. However, do ask the college about exceptions such as if you are in receipt of benefits.

Not all FE colleges have nurseries on campus, though many do, so you will need to consider how and where your child will be cared for and if you will have enough time to commute between home, nursery and college.

Short-term courses

These are ideal if you want to brush up your skills, develop a new hobby or have a taste of the topic in preparation for a longer course. What makes short-term courses particularly appealing to many parents is that the time commitment is only for a short period of time, ideal if you are unsure whether you can commit to something longer.

Some short courses are free, depending on the type of course and your household income. Some will be payable and fees should be clearly set out at the start of the course. Short courses might offer a certificate to say that you have taken the course or they might offer a qualification from a recognised body.

Access courses

These courses are designed for mature students who want to progress on to higher education. There are many different Access courses available, in specific or general topics, and they each lead to a recognised qualification. The course can be taken over one year on a full-time basis, and in some cases part-time spread out over two years.

People who choose this type of course tend not to have any other qualifications, such as GCSEs or A-levels, but do aim to go on to university. Alongside learning about specific topics, students on Access courses will also be helped with study skills and eased back in to good classroom practice.

You are never too old to start an Access course. You can find more information about what Access courses are available in your area from www.ucas.com or www.accesstohe.co.uk.

Higher education

Universities aren't just for 18-year-olds. A significant proportion of the student body is made up of 'mature students', over the age of 21, who are studying for BAs, BSCs and more. Mature students are often thought to be more focused than younger students because they have had the time, and the life experiences, to really consider what they want to do with their lives and are now determined to take the steps to get there.

Many younger parents, such as those who have had children while in their teens, may feel that university is barred to them due to the pressures of raising a young child while pursuing an education. It may be more challenging, and there will be more to deal with than your peers, especially in terms of looking after your child. However, many young parents have found that attending university whilst their child is young has proven beneficial to them. Young parents cite examples, such as they had more energy to pursue education and look after their child, that they were already used to having little money so student living did not seem like a step backwards. Many say that by the time their child was at school they had raised their family's prospects by gaining a degree. Young parents may also have the option of attending university closer to home which may make juggling their commitments easier.

All students should check their eligibility for means-tested grants and loans to cover tuition fees and some costs, though this will not solely cover a family's living expenses and any money you may be entitled to will be dependent on your family's income. You will also be liable to pay back monies borrowed just as any other student would.

Postgraduate education

This comprises of the highest level of qualifications you can achieve; MAs, MSCs, MBAs, Mphils and PhDs, along with other diplomas. By now you will already have achieved qualifications up to degree level and may be well versed in the rigours of study. You may have also had time in the workplace and have built up a good CV.

Reasons for taking up postgraduate study vary. It might fit in well with your role in bringing up your child, you might have taken time out to have children and want to brush up skills to put yourself back in a strong position when returning to the workplace or help you change career direction. You might even be looking for something to do that works well alongside childcare, and stops those feelings of your brain melting after looking after children.

Your prospective course tutor will inform you about funding options for the course you want to take. Postgraduate funding is limited and competition for resources from funding bodies is intense. As such, many postgraduate students fund their courses themselves and these costs should be given thought before committing to a course.

Distance learning

If there isn't a course or institution close to home that interests you, you may be able to find a distance-learning course. A note of warning though, thoroughly research the institution before you hand over any funds. Ask yourself:

- Is the institution a recognised education provider?

- Does the course give a recognised qualification that an employer will appreciate?

- Is the course value for money?

- Will it add anything to your CV or general interests?

- Is the course unrealistic in what it is offering?

There are institutions out there who offer qualifications that are meaningless and they should be avoided – with good research this shouldn't be a problem.

The Open University is the largest long-distance learning provider in the country, with a large campus in Milton Keynes. They offer undergraduate and postgraduate degrees along with a multitude of diplomas and shorter courses. Learning can be spread out over a number of years or courses can be taken concurrently, depending on how much time you are prepared to devote to study on top of your day-to-day life. They do charge fees and qualifications are recognised worldwide. First-time students taking first level courses can apply for funding to help with course fees.

How should you study?

Generally, courses can be split into full-time or part-time study. At university level, full-time study tends not to mean that you will be in classes for an entire day. Instead your day might consist of a small number of lectures and seminars with plenty of free time for studying and other activities. Part-time study takes the same classes but spread out over a longer period of time and requires less class and study time per week. There are pros and cons for each group which we explore below.

Pros of part-time courses

- Part-time courses give you the flexibility to manage both your daily life and study.

- There is less pressure as classes and coursework are spread out.

- You may be able to spread payments, if required.
- It eases you back into education

Cons of part-time courses

- Courses take longer to complete.
- You might lose enthusiasm over a longer period of time.
- You may incur additional costs in living expenses by spreading the study.
- If you need to leave your course, you probably won't get a refund or qualification.

Pros of full-time courses

- You will finish your course faster.
- You can concentrate fully on your studies.
- You may become more absorbed in student life.
- Getting qualifications sooner may mean reaching your goals sooner.

Cons of full-time courses

- You may not have time to hold down a job as well as study.
- You may be taking courses concurrently so have to study a range of topics.
- It might be more expensive for paid for courses.
- You might find it difficult to manage study, childcare and work.

'Long-distance learning is an excellent way of studying and one that really does mean that nearly anyone can join up.'
Julia, 29, Open University.

Case study

Julia, 29, Open University.

'Studying long distance was a way that I could exercise my brain whilst being stuck at home with a small baby. I managed to keep hold of part of my identity by doing those courses, almost like "me time". It was also a constructive thing that I was able to do while I was at home with my boy and something that I could stick on my CV or tell future employers. I made sure that wherever I could, I'd involve my boy in my studies, like reading aloud to him, and talking to him about what I was studying and doing, even when he was a baby.

At the time, I was eligible for help towards the cost of the courses I did. I had to apply for this via the Open University student support people. Depending on the number of credits of the course people can apply for different things, including grants towards computers and broadband. Of course, this financial help is means-tested and also dependent on whether you have kids and dependants or are on any benefits.

The beauty of these courses is that you don't have to literally be at university. You do them from home and in your own time. I started with the OU when my son was tiny – he was just a month old – so most of the time he'd be on my lap and I'd be reading aloud from textbooks. There was a double benefit there, he'd have interaction and hear my voice while I got my studies done! I'm lucky because I enjoy studying, it never really was a chore for me but you do have to be disciplined and make sure you do what you can, when you can. If I needed to study something without interruptions, I'd make sure I did what I could during the day and then do the more hardcore stuff once my son was having a nap, or in bed for the night. Long-distance learning is an excellent way of studying and one that really does mean that nearly anyone can join up.'

Summing Up

■ There are many different types of paths to an education and you should visit colleges and ask for brochures and prospectuses so you can find the right course for you.

■ If you get the education bug, there are many opportunities for progression once you've taken, and passed, that first class.

■ Many courses have varying degrees of flexibility so you can find one that allows you a balanced home and study life.

■ Long-distance learning is an ideal way of taking up a course without commuting or even having to be on campus.

■ Education is open to everyone. All you have to do is have a little faith in yourself.

Chapter Ten

Postgraduate Study

Well done! You've run the gamut of qualifications and will already have had a taste of university life while doing your previous degree. Now you may be considering becoming one of the 140,000 studying for a Masters or one of the 90,000 undertaking a PhD in their specialist subject every year (Swain, 2010).

By now you will be well versed in the ins and outs of studying, but you may be wondering how you can combine postgraduate study with family life or a pregnancy.

Impact of postgraduate study on family life

Postgraduate students tend to be 'mature' students. That is, already past 21 years old with a raft of qualifications under your belt. You may already have settled in to a career, have a house and have started a family of one or more children. Becoming a student again after having a career can certainly be an attractive prospect and it is often a more flexible choice when you have children to consider.

Knowing that they have already successfully combined family life and work, will often be encouraging for the parents who want to return to study. Many postgraduate students treat their further studies in the same way as they would a job, by keeping regular hours, defining time for study and keeping on top of commitments to their families. Similarly, they may already have a home and a well-rounded social life so may not be looking to access the stereotypical undergraduate lifestyle again. That's not to say there aren't important points to consider. Postgraduate parents may have to be prepared for extra financial commitments, reduced earnings and more draws on their time than before.

'The postgraduate community is, in my experience, more diverse, so I found it easier to make friends with my fellow students than I did as an undergraduate. They're more understanding of the situation facing student parents and often organise events with partners and children in mind.'

Claire, 33, PhD Politics.

Benefits of postgraduate study

- Might help if you want to change your career, improve salary, and want to boost your CV.

- It might mean a more flexible lifestyle, giving you more time with your children.

- You can refresh skills, or get new ones, after a period out of your career, like taking time out to have children.

- Give yourself extra time to re-enter the job market, or avoid periods of instability in the job market.

- You may have already had a lot of practical experience in the study area.

Things to consider

- Funding is often limited for postgraduate courses so you may have to pay your own fees. Or, your employer or university might sponsor you.

- You may have to juggle children, family, work and study, especially when there are imminent deadlines or exams.

- There might be an impact on your living expenses if you need to take time out from your career for a year or several years.

- Try to define a plan for how you wish your studies and career to proceed, including realistic timescales and prospects. Will the course help you work towards that?

- Carefully consider which university offers the course you want, whether it is commutable and what support, if any, they will offer you.

Full-time, part-time or distance learning?

Generally, postgraduate study can be carried out on a full-time or part-time basis, which can be helpful if you are also combining work with family life. Both have benefits, for example, full-time courses are completed quicker enabling you to move on to the next step, whereas part-time courses can work well with other time-heavy commitments. Let's look at the pros and cons of each.

Pros of full-time study

■ You will complete the course faster and therefore be able to return to work in the shortest time possible.

■ The course fees will be more expensive in the short term, but living expenses won't be drawn out over a longer period of time.

Cons of full-time study

■ You may be pressed for time due to commitments to study and family life.

■ You may have to leave your job to meet full-time study commitments.

Pros of part-time study

■ You will have a reduced study load so it could be easier to combine with family and work.

■ The course fees will be reduced fees in the short term, however the full fee is still payable in the long term.

Cons of part-time study

■ Your course will take longer to complete, which could have implications for living expenses and career plans.

■ Your initial enthusiasm might be reduced or lost during prolonged study.

Pros of distance learning

■ You might be able to take an accredited course that is not available locally.

■ You might be able to continue working and be able to build your study hours around other commitments, such as children.

Cons of distance learning

■ You will miss out on the social side of university as well as lacking face-to-face time with tutors and on-site access to a university library.

■ You will have to be extremely self-motivated and organised.

How to apply

Applying for postgraduate study isn't as straightforward as undergraduate study where applications are consolidated via UCAS. Instead, you will generally apply to each university or department individually for their course prospectus and application guidelines. You will have to list your current qualifications to show that you are of an appropriate standard to meet the course entry requirements. You will also be asked for references. If you have recently completed undergraduate study, you should approach your tutor to ask if they would provide a reference. If it is some time since you studied, you should be able to ask an employer for a reference.

In your application form you might be asked to provide the reasons why you want to undertake the course. This should demonstrate your enthusiasm for the topic as well as your knowledge and intention to stay the course. Don't be tempted to write the same for multiple applications. Tailor each statement for the individual university.

Prospective PhD candidates will be asked to submit a research proposal for their topic. Your proposal will generally include:

■ Hypothesis – what you propose to do.

■ Literature review – what other people have written on the topic and why it's different to what you will do.

- Methodology – how you will do the research to answer your hypothesis.

- What will you do with the research – how will it help your career and the university? How it will make a difference in the wider topic area.

- Conclusion – summing up everything you have said.

The proposal should demonstrate that you have thoughtfully considered your topic and can research and present an original piece of work. This does not have to be the finished proposal. You might be invited to meet with prospective tutors in an interview-type meeting where you will discuss the proposed research and hone the proposal. During this meeting funding options might be discussed, but you should be aware competition for funding at this level is intense.

You might have applied for an advertised research post. In this case, the post will already have a specified research topic leading to a qualification. Generally funding will be in place, though it should be noted that what is on offer is usually not enough to singularly support a family. Therefore, if you are offered a funded post, you should check to see if you can access tax and childcare credits.

Funding postgraduate study

Finding funding for postgraduate study is not easy. There are funding boards along with studentships from universities, but they are few and far between, with intense competition for each place. Some employers may also fund postgraduate study if it can be proved that the additional qualification will be of benefit to the company.

It is, of course, possible to self-fund your tuition fees and living expenses and many students do this. Some sources of funding for UK students include:

University funds

In some cases, Universities may have financial resources set aside to pay for all of, or part of, your fees or contribute towards living expenses by the way of bursaries. Competition for these funds will be intense with less funds than there are applicants. You may also be eligible, in special cases, for hardship funds available through the university's welfare or finance offices.

Research councils

There are seven research councils that are government funded and provide funding for postgraduate study. These include the Economic and Social Research Council (ESRC), Arts and Humanities Research Council (AHRC) and Science and Technology Facilities Council (STFC). Each council covers a different set of research areas although there is occasionally some overlap. Entry requirements vary and, once again, competition is intense.

Professional and Career Development Loans

These funds are provided via some of the major high street banks. Prospective students can apply for funds to pay towards course and living expenses. Funds are then paid back at the end of the course whether you have completed it or not. They are often offered for vocational or shorter-taught courses, though that is not always the rule.

MBAs

MBA loans operate in a similar way to Career Development Loans. They are provided by high street banks to pay for fees and course materials. You will still need to contribute towards costs and you will need to have had several years of work experience. MBA studentships may also be available and you should check with the university you are interested in.

Studentships

Many universities create studentship posts in research areas they are particularly interested in. There is generally a small stipend and course fees paid with the work leading to a qualification. Studentships are often advertised via university jobs sections, including online, and the application process will be similar to that of a regular job.

Employers

Many businesses sponsor their employers to take up further qualifications as this enhances both the company and the employee. They will often pay course fees and allow time out from work in which to study or attend class.

Self-funding

Many students find funding inaccessible for postgraduate study and choose to fund their courses themselves. This can be a combination of savings, family funds or loans, partner contribution with living expenses supported by work, family or savings.

These are not the only funding options available and you should thoroughly assess your finances and research what might be available. Fees are generally non-refundable so you should be determined to finish before committing to a course. To find more information about funding visit: www.scholarship-search. org.uk, www.prospects.ac.uk and www.rcuk.ac.uk.

Finding time

Time is one of your most valuable commodities whilst at university. Think of the days when you had a study chart leading up to exams, or a school timetable, and divide your day up in a similar manner.

	Mon	Tues	Wed	Thurs	Fri	Sat	Sun
7:00							
8:00							
9:00							
10:00							
11:00							
12:00							
13:00							
14:00							
15:00							
16:00							
17:00							
18:00							
19:00							
20:00							
21:00							
22:00							
23:00							

Start with the days of the week and then divide each day into hourly slots. Immediately rule out the time you'll be asleep. Rule out other times when you will not be able to study, such as through work commitments. Include time for commuting if necessary. Look at the time you have left. Is there enough time for a reasonable amount of study? If there is, then you could reasonably consider taking a course.

Consider when you will have reliable childcare and if there is anyone (such as a partner or parents) who will regularly take on childcare for some time on weekends.

Remember that time commitments can change. You may find you need more or less time for study.

How to be well prepared

By this stage, you will already be aware of the commitment and time studying requires, so it will not come as a shock that there will be many hours of reading, researching and writing, on top of making dinner, playing and bedtime stories. However, if you completed your previous qualifications without having children, you might be concerned about how to combine the two.

Organisation is a key part of successfully doing and completing your postgraduate degree. You will need to allot yourself time in which to study, research and prepare material, just as you would use effective time management at work.

Draw up a plan that will cover the length of your course. A multiyear calendar could work – mark off holiday periods and key dates for assessments.

Don't leave things until the last minute. Give yourself plenty of time to meet course commitments so that you aren't stressed at the last moment. That way if your child is ill or there are any last minute urgent things to do, you will already have started and may even be ahead.

Tell your children what you are doing. Young children might not 'get it' but older children will appreciate knowing why you are studying, when you are doing it and when it will end.

Case study

Rachel, 27, full-time PhD research student.

'I was a few weeks into my PhD programme when I realised I was pregnant. Having children has made me even more motivated and determined to get that PhD, because I now feel I have something to prove. Many people asked me, "Can you have a baby and do a PhD at the same time?" when I told them about my pregnancy. Having children has influenced my outlook, my academic interests and made me a fighter. Being a pregnant student raised a few eyebrows and being a working from home student parent has left me very detached and isolated from the university experience as a whole – something I previously really embraced.

I took six months maternity leave from my studies, and although I felt very guilty when I returned to the books, putting such a young baby in nursery twice a week so I could have two full days of reading, I felt like part of me had returned. I was very lucky to receive a full stipend for the period of five years, which pays my study fees and gives me a maintenance allowance to live from. I am classed as a student, so don't pay tax. This sounds ideal, but no, it means I'm not entitled to any help towards my childcare costs. My baby often comes with me when I'm interviewing people for my research and I regularly study in the evenings and when I'm pushing the baby round the park in the afternoons I think about ideas and concepts. My supervisors think my work is better thought through than previously.

Having children is not an obstacle to studying, as they can really enrich your work, just like they enrich your life.'

Case study

Heidi, 28, MA, Public Communication and PR.

'I fell pregnant during my course and was five months pregnant by the end. I told my tutors after my three-month scan and they were very supportive. I'd planned the pregnancy so as to ensure I'd have finished the course long before the baby arrived so it never seemed like that much of a big deal in terms of any impact on my studying. I was tired during those first three months – but the prospect of having a baby was hugely motivating for keeping me focused on getting my dissertation done.

One reason for doing the course was because we were ready to have a family and I knew, all being well, that I'd be having some time off from my career so I saw the course as an investment in my longer-term future. That's probably why I was so at ease with being a pregnant student but other people definitely seemed to see it as a bit of an anomaly. I never really thought of it as a big deal that I was pregnant and studying then graduating.

I was about five months pregnant when my course finished. My friends were out toasting their freedom and looking forward to the summer off after an intensive year of studying, meanwhile I was sipping soft drinks and unwrapping tiny baby grows! My graduation ceremony was three weeks before my due date and my tutor offered me a job as a part-time visiting lecturer after I graduated.'

'The prospect of having a baby was hugely motivating for keeping me focused on getting my dissertation done.'

Heidi, 28, MA, Public Communication and PR.

Summing Up

- Committing to postgraduate study is like committing to a job – treat it seriously by keeping regular hours, being prepared and being focused.

- There are many benefits to postgraduate study, including career improvement, enjoyment, a better work/life balance and showing your children how beneficial study is.

- Many universities are much more flexible about postgraduate study now. You can often choose between full-time, part-time and distance learning, depending on what suits you.

- All students should carefully research their institution and tailor each application to that course provider.

- Funding is notoriously intense for postgraduate study. You should research funding options as early as possible and consider whether it is affordable to pay all or some of your course fees and living expenses.

- Good organisation and preparation is crucial to keeping a good study/work/ life balance. Plan ahead, know what you need to do and never leave things to the last minute.

Chapter Eleven

Tips for Academic Success

NUS research (2009) indicates that student parents are amongst the most likely student group to consider that 'failure is not an option'. This chapter offers practical tips and advice for getting the most out of their study.

Exams, coursework or both

At the end of every course you take, there will generally be an assessment to find out how much you have learned and the mark you receive will generally go towards your final grade.

Assessments can take the form of an exam or an essay, sometimes in conjunction with an assessment of coursework carried out throughout the course. Whether your final assessment is an exam or essay depends on the type of course you take. Generally, you will be told at the start of the course how the marking will be conducted. You may also be offered a list of topics that will be covered in the exam or be given a list of essay titles to choose from which will help you with your revision schedule.

You might find you particularly excel at exams and so gravitate towards classes where exams count the most towards your final course mark. Alternatively, you might find essays are your thing.

The bonus of essays is that you can take more time over them and don't have to worry about a sleepless night the night before. On the other hand, exams are completed in a few hours.

Note-taking and revision skills

Initially, note-taking can be a 'hit and miss' type of activity as students struggle to make snap decisions on what is the most important piece of information to record during a lecture. However, it is these notes that will often form the basis of your revision later so it is important to get in to good practise from the beginning. Take good notes by:

- Being prepared with enough paper, pens or pencils.

- Head up each set of notes with the class, topic, lecturer and date to make it easy to refer to and find later.

- Listen to what your lecturer has to say and really pay attention, instead of letting your mind wander.

- Use abbreviations and symbols where possible, making sure that you can recognise what they mean. This is especially useful for long or frequent words.

- Leave spaces so that you have visual breaks between notes and can also add supplementary information later for anything you have missed or not understood.

- Don't write down everything. You don't need a transcription, just key facts, statistics and points.

- Take any handouts offered to supplement your own notes.

- Type up your notes later. This will give you an electronic back-up, a clean-looking set of notes (i.e. without scrawls, scribbles and crossings out) plus reading them through and typing up will help you process the information.

- Read your notes as soon as possible after class and highlight any particularly important parts or make notes to ask further questions or to read more around the topic.

- File in a binder with notes from the same class so you can find all your notes later.

Study tips

Studying is a vital part of your education. It will give you the opportunity to go over your coursework notes again and help you consolidate the information you have learned during your course. This helps when you have to take an exam or write an essay for assessment. In the same way that you will learn a new topic, you will learn how to study and which methods work best for you.

Good study tips

- Don't cram – instead revise topics in advance so that you have a thorough understanding.

- Make a timetable – know when your final assessment is and work out how much study time you will need prior to this. Make sure you have enough time to cover all your topics, including extra time for any areas you aren't confident in.

- Revise alone – having children or family members around generally equals constant interruptions which is not conducive to learning and retaining information.

- Test yourself – at the end of each study session, ask yourself 'what are the most important points I have learned?' What statistics and facts can you recall? Do you know any quotes off by heart?

- Set up your study zone – get everything ready that you will need when studying. Pens, paper, note cards, text books, drink, snack? Check! Good preparation will stop you being distracted when you are supposed to be working.

- Little and often – don't plan major study sessions. Instead study for 30 minute blocks.

- Rewards – don't forget to give yourself a treat at the end of study so you have something to look forward to, such as a walk in the park, a bar of chocolate or your favourite TV show. Whatever you will look forward to will work as an incentive.

Writing and planning essays

There are plenty of books dedicated to the art of essay writing, but most boil down to a few simple rules to ensure that you turn in the essay you have been assigned to write:

- Stay on topic – don't deviate from the subject you are supposed to be writing

- Have a start, middle and end. Introduce your argument, prove it and conclude it, accounting for how you have made your argument.

- Consider the sources – which books and article excerpts support your argument? Have you cited them correctly?

- Start early – when you have children you can't leave essay writing to the last minute.

- Meet the word count – some places offer a leeway of 10% of the total words under or over, but you could lose marks for not turning in the right number of words.

- Use your spell checker – then proofread the essay to make sure the spell checker got it right.

- Some of these rules can also apply during an exam situation – although you won't have source material on hand to quote, you will be expected to know your topics and be able to make a convincing argument in a structured essay.

The importance of seminars, lectures and study groups

It can be tempting to miss seminars or lectures, but they are valuable learning time and each have a different way of imparting information.

Lectures

Lectures will often be the first time you are introduced to a topic. During a lecture, your lecturer will generally stand at the front of a classroom and talk through a pre-prepared presentation. The talk might also include the use of aids, such as PowerPoint presentations, demonstrations or handouts to give a visual angle to the topic. There will be many other students in your lecture and they will often be held in dedicated lecture spaces, often with tiered seating so everyone can see what is going on. You should always arrive a few minutes early as some lecturers will not admit latecomers as it could be disruptive for others.

Most students miss the occasional lecture and if you need to, you will need to find a way to gain the information. With advance discussion with your lecturer you might be able to leave a Dictaphone to record the lecture so you can listen to it later. Many electronic Dictaphones can upload sound files straight to your computer. These are useful because they give you a permanent record that you can listen to later. Your lecturer might also send you lecture notes or handouts or instruct you where to find further reading. If you know people in the class, they might be willing to let you look over their notes.

Try not to make a habit out of missing lectures. They are important for you to build your knowledge of the topic.

Seminars and classes

Seminars are generally compulsory and will usually occur the same week in which the co-ordinating lecture is given. Seminars are held in smaller groups and are an opportunity to show what information you have learned. Students might work together in small groups or individually and might be asked to prepare presentations, hold debates or do other work to further their knowledge. It's also a good time for seminar leaders to give more information and for students to ask any questions they might have.

If you frequently don't attend classes you will be asked to explain why and may fail the course through lack of attendance. You should inform your course leader in advance if you know you won't make the class and ask what you can do to keep up.

Study groups

Students might set up their own study groups in addition to lectures and seminars. They aren't compulsory, but you might find it useful to look at each other's notes and informally discuss the topic. This can help to fill any gaps in your own knowledge as well as help revise the topic.

Sometimes your lecturer might host a study group and it is always a good idea to go along if you can so that you can, ask any more questions.

Asking for help

Many people see asking for help as a sign of weakness, but if you don't ask for help when you need it, you can't expect other people to know that you need help. Asking for help is a pre-emptive way of getting help in order to meet your commitments rather than floundering at the last possible moment.

So, if your child has chickenpox and will need to be at home when you are trying to meet a deadline, let your tutor know and ask if you can have an extension. Do remember that you might be asked to prove why you need extra time to combat those who make up excuses.

'Don't be afraid to ask for help from family or friends. Even if they can only take your little one to the shops for half an hour make the most of that, read up on the subject you need to write about, write an essay plan, take every available opportunity and don't worry about the housework!'

Hayley, 20, Access to Social Sciences.

Summing Up

- Plan ahead – know when your assessments are and mark them on your calendar so you can prepare well in advance.

- Get past papers – these will help you recognise assessment type questions and practise them in the time allotted.

- Realise where your strengths and weaknesses lie. If you work well under exam conditions, look for exam-based classes, and vice versa if you perform better with coursework assessments.

- Reward yourself – you've taken your last test for that topic. Give yourself a 'well done' treat. Not only is it something to look forward to but it is positive reinforcement.

Help List

Access to HE

www.accesstohe.ac.uk
Access to HE courses are designed for people who would like to study at university but who left school without the usual qualifications, such as A-levels.

Barnardo's

www.barnardos.org.uk
Support, training and advice for young people along with published research focusing on helping teen mums return to education.

Brightside UNIAID

CAN Mezzanine, Downstream Building, 1 London Bridge, London, SE1 9BG
Tel: 0207 785 3894
www.uniaid.org.uk
Support for 14-25 year-olds with information about education, money and careers. They have lots of guidance for student parents transferring from further to higher education, including study skills, budgeting, childcare and university life, plus a mentoring scheme.

British Mummy Bloggers (studying parents group)

www.britishmummybloggers.ning.com/group/studyingparents
Online support group for parents who study with links to other parenting groups.

Childcare Link

www.childcarelink.gov.uk
Government-run website with a postcode finder for childcare providers in that area.

Citizens Advice Bureau

www.citizensadvice.org.uk

UK-wide service offering free and impartial advice on a variety of matters, such as housing, employment, benefits and education.

Connexions Direct

Tel: 080 800 13 2 19

www.connexions-direct.com

Information and advice for 13-19 year-olds on issues including careers, learning and money.

Daycare Trust

2nd Floor, Novas Contemporary Urban Centre, 73-81 Southwark Bridge Road, London, SE1 ONQ

Tel: 0845 872 6251

www.daycaretrust.org.uk

National childcare charity campaigning for quality, accessible and affordable childcare for all.

Department for Education

www.education.gov.uk

Government-run website with information for, and about, local authorities, teachers, parents and young people.

Department for Employment and Education (Northern Ireland)

Tel: 028 9025 7777

www.delni.gov.uk

Information for Northern Ireland residents on further and higher education.

DirectGov

www.direct.gov.uk

Government-run site with lots of information about going to university, student finance and parenting. The website also has a postcode finder for local authorities. You will also find all the information you need on: Child Benefit, Tax Credits, Childcare Tax Credits, Housing Benefit, Income Support, Access to Learning Fund, Childcare Grants and the Parents' Learning Allowance.

Family Action

430 Highgate Studios, 53-79 Highgate Road, London, NW5 1TL
Tel: 020 7424 3460
www.family-action.org.uk
Provider of the Educational Grants Programme (EGAS) aimed at low-income families and individuals, including those on benefits.

Gingerbread

255 Kentish Town Road, London, NW5 2LX
Tel: 0808 8020925
www.gingerbread.org.uk
Charity focusing on single parents' rights with aims to improve the lives of single parent families and to give them a voice without labels.

GotaTeenager

Tel: 0808 800 2222
www.gotateenager.org.uk
Operated by Parentline Plus, this website offers informal advice and information for parents of teenagers.

HM Revenue and Customs

www.hmrc.gov.uk
Government advice and application forms for Child Benefit and tax credits.

Horizons

Horizons Education Fund, Family Action, 501-505 Kingsland Road, London, E8 4AU
Tel: 020 7254 6251
www.yourhorizons.com
Advice on money, education and work for single parents. Also offers Horizons Your Education grant.

Independent Schools Council

www.isc.co.uk
Search this website for independent childcare options.

Learn Direct

Tel: 0800 101 901

www.learndirect.co.uk

Large e-learning provider with lots of courses and qualifications to study for.

Learner Support Helpline

Tel: 0800 121 8989

www.direct.gov.uk

This helpline offers advice on a variety of financial awards including: Education Maintenance Allowance (EMA), Care to Learn, the Sixth Form College Childcare Scheme, Adult Learning Grant (ALG) and the Free Childcare for Training and Learning for Work Scheme.

National Institute of Adults Continuing Education (NIACE)

20 Princess Road West, Leicester, LE1 6TP

Tel: 0116 204 4200

www.niace.org.uk

NIACE promotes adult learning and campaigns on behalf of adult learners. They also run an annual adult learners' week and have advice for those working with learners.

National Union of Students (NUS)

NUS HQ, Centro 3, 19 Mandela Street, London, SW1 ODU

Tel: 0207 380 6600

www.nus.org.uk

Union for all university students in the UK with research and advice on many issues affecting students.

Netmums

www.netmums.com

A family of local sites that cover the UK, each site offering information to mothers on everything from where to find playgroups and how to eat healthily, to where to meet other mothers.

Nuffield Foundation

Tel: 020 7631 0566
www.nuffieldfoundation.org
Independent funding for research with information about grants.

Open University (OU)

Tel: 0845 300 60 90
www.open.ac.uk
Distance-learning university with a wide variety of courses including undergraduate and postgraduate degrees. Courses can be taken at the learner's own pace and from home with regular face-to-face local study sessions as agreed. They have financial awards on offer to help towards some course fees and other study costs.

ParentlinePlus

Tel: 0808 800 2222
www.parentlineplus.org.uk
National charity for anyone involved in parenting and the issues families face.

Paying for Childcare (Daycare Trust)

www.payingforchildcare.org.uk
Website from Daycare Trust that will help you to understand the financial support you may be able to receive for childcare costs.

Prospects

www.prospects.ac.uk
Website with some information about funding postgraduate study. It also has lots of information about careers, jobs and being a student.

Scholarship Search

www.scholarship-search.org.uk
Website with information about funding that might be available to you to help with expenses.

Straight Talking

Tel: 020 8605 0900
www.straighttalking.org
National teenage pregnancy charity with peer-to-peer support for young parents to move into education, employment and training.

Student Awards Agency (Scotland)

Gyleview House, 3 Redheughs Rigg, Edinburgh, EH12 9HH
Tel: 0845 111 1711
www.student-support-saas.gov.uk
Awards body for tuition fees, loans and grants for higher education courses in Scotland.

Student Finance England

www.studentfinance.direct.gov.uk
Information and application forms for applying for student loans, grants and bursaries in England.

Student Finance Northern Ireland

Tel: 0845 600 0662
www.studentfinanceni.co.uk
Information and advice for students from Northern Ireland.

Student Finance Wales

Tel: 0845 602 8845
www.studentfinancewales.co.uk
Information and services for students in Wales.

Student Loan Repayment

Tel: 0845 026 2019
www.studentloanrepayment.co.uk
Information about repaying loans for students in England, Scotland, Wales and Northern Ireland.

Student Parents – The Essential Guide

www.studentparentsguide.com
Website to accompany this book with links, information, case studies and more information.

Student Parents Network

http://studentparentsnetwork.blogspot.com
For student parents, by student parents, this website has information and support for parents continuing their education.

Sure Start Maternity Grant

www.direct.gov.uk
One-off payment of £500 from the government to help cover the costs of a new baby. Applicants need to be claiming qualifying Child Tax Credits or qualifying benefits.

The Grants Register

www.palgrave.com
Annual book with details of all funding and grant opportunities for postgraduate study. It's very expensive so see if your local library or university has access to a copy.

TheSchoolRun

www.theschoolrun.com
A good place to look for socialising and networking with other mums.

The Site

www.thesite.org
Huge amount of information and advice for young people on issues including education, sex and relationships, money and health and wellbeing.

Turn2Us

Tel: 0808 802 2000

www.turn2us.org.uk

Independent charity helping people find and access welfare benefits and grants.

UCAS

Tel: 0871 468 0468

www.ucas.ac.uk

Everything you will need to apply to university: search for university courses, make applications, find out what offers have been made and if the application is successful.

Young Mums

www.youngmums.org.uk

Information and advice for mothers under the age of 20 and resident in Northern Ireland, including education, health and welfare benefits. There is also some information about the School Age Mother Project on this website.

YWCA

Clarendon House, 52 Cornmarket Street, Oxford, OX1 3EJ

Tel: 01865 304200

www.ywca.org.uk

Charity working with disadvantaged young women and girls aged from 11-30. Information includes employment, education and skills.

References

Department for Children Schools and Families/Department of Education, *Teenage Pregnancy: Statistics*, www.dcsf.gov.uk/everychildmatters/ healthandwellbeing/teenagepregnancy/statistics/statistics/, accessed 3 August 2010.

Duncan, S *et al.*, *Teenage Parenthood: What's the Problem?*, Tufnell Press, London, 2010.

Evans, J, *Not the end of the story: Supporting teenage mothers back in to education*, Barnardo's, London, 2010, www.barnardos.org.uk/12210_pru_teen_report.pdf, accessed 3 August 2010.

Smith, G and Wayman, S, *Meet the Parents*, NUS, London, 2009.

Swain, H, 'How research degrees lead to greater employability', *Guardian*, 2010, www.guardian.co.uk/education/2010/mar/16/research-degrees-lead-to-greater-employability, accessed 3 August 2010.

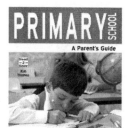
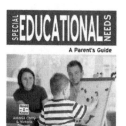
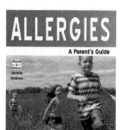

Need - 2 - Know

Available Titles Include ...

Allergies A Parent's Guide
ISBN 978-1-86144-064-8 £8.99

Autism A Parent's Guide
ISBN 978-1-86144-069-3 £8.99

Blood Pressure The Essential Guide
ISBN 978-1-86144-067-9 £8.99

Dyslexia and Other Learning Difficulties
A Parent's Guide ISBN 978-1-86144-042-6 £8.99

Bullying A Parent's Guide
ISBN 978-1-86144-044-0 £8.99

Epilepsy The Essential Guide
ISBN 978-1-86144-063-1 £8.99

Your First Pregnancy The Essential Guide
ISBN 978-1-86144-066-2 £8.99

Gap Years The Essential Guide
ISBN 978-1-86144-079-2 £8.99

Secondary School A Parent's Guide
ISBN 978-1-86144-093-8 £9.99

Primary School A Parent's Guide
ISBN 978-1-86144-088-4 £9.99

Applying to University The Essential Guide
ISBN 978-1-86144-052-5 £8.99

ADHD The Essential Guide
ISBN 978-1-86144-060-0 £8.99

Student Cookbook – Healthy Eating The Essential Guide
ISBN 978-1-86144-069-3 £8.99

Multiple Sclerosis The Essential Guide
ISBN 978-1-86144-086-0 £8.99

Coeliac Disease The Essential Guide
ISBN 978-1-86144-087-7 £9.99

Special Educational Needs A Parent's Guide
ISBN 978-1-86144-116-4 £9.99

The Pill An Essential Guide
ISBN 978-1-86144-058-7 £8.99

University A Survival Guide
ISBN 978-1-86144-072-3 £8.99

View the full range at **www.need2knowbooks.co.uk**.
To order our titles call **01733 898103**, email **sales@ n2kbooks.com** or visit the website. Selected ebooks available online.

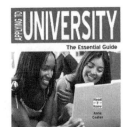
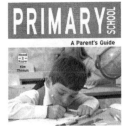

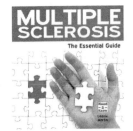

Need - 2 - Know, Remus House, Coltsfoot Drive, Peterborough, PE2 9JX